Environmental Security in the Arctic Ocean
Promoting Co-operation and Preventing Conflict

Paul Arthur Berkman

www.rusi.org

Royal United Services Institute for Defence and Security Studies

Environmental Security in the Arctic Ocean: Promoting Co-operation and Preventing Conflict
By Paul Arthur Berkman
First published 2010

Whitehall Papers series

Series Editor: Professor Malcolm Chalmers
Editors: Adrian Johnson and Anna Rader
Editorial Assistant: Lindsay O'Sullivan

RUSI is a registered charity (no. 210639)
ISBN 0855161531

Published on behalf of the Royal United Services Institute
for Defence and Security Studies
by
Routledge Journals, an imprint of Taylor & Francis, 4 Park Square, Milton Park, Abingdon OX14 4RN

SUBSCRIPTIONS
Please send subscription orders to:

USA/Canada: Taylor & Francis Inc., Journals Department, 325 Chestnut Street, 8th Floor, Philadelphia, PA 19106 USA

UK/Rest of World: Routledge Journals, T&F Customer Services, T&F Informa UK Ltd, Sheepen Place, Colchester, Essex, CO3 3LP, UK

All rights reserved. No part of this publication may be reprinted or reproduced or utilised in any form or by any electronic, mechanical, or other means, now known or hereafter invented, including photocopying and recording, or in any information storage or retrieval system, without permission in writing from the publisher.

Contents

About the Author iv
Acknowledgements vi
Acronyms and Abbreviations vii

Foreword viii

1. **Introduction** 1

2. **The Arctic Ocean** 10

3. **Beyond National Boundaries** 30

4. **Matters of Security** 52

5. **Arctic Ocean Stewardship** 88

6. **Global Statesmanship** 110

About the Author

Paul Arthur Berkman is Head of the Arctic Ocean Geopolitics Programme at the Scott Polar Research Institute at the University of Cambridge, and a Research Professor at the Bren School of Environmental Science and Management at the University of California, Santa Barbara. He is an oceanographer working on interdisciplinary connections between science, policy and information technology to promote co-operation and prevent conflict in the Arctic Ocean, Antarctica and regions beyond sovereign jurisdictions more generally. His science diplomacy activities involve: balancing national interests and common interests in the Arctic Ocean, assessing science policy lessons from the Antarctic Treaty System, and considering the role of international spaces in global governance for the lasting benefit of all life on Earth.

Professor Berkman has wintered in Antarctica, scuba dived under the sea ice and led government-sponsored research expeditions to the continent. He has a master's degree and doctorate in biological oceanography from the University of Rhode Island, where he was a National Science Foundation (NSF) Graduate Fellow. He also has received: the Antarctic Service Medal from the United States Congress; the National Aeronautics and Space Administration (NASA) Faculty Fellowship at the Jet Propulsion Laboratory, California Institute of Technology; the Byrd Fellowship at the Byrd Polar Research Center, Ohio State University; the Japan Society for the Promotion of Science (JSPS) Fellowship at the National Institute of Polar Research in Tokyo; the Erskine Fellowship at Gateway Antarctica, University of Canterbury, New Zealand; and a Fulbright Distinguished Scholarship in the United Kingdom at the University of Cambridge.

His interdisciplinary research is reflected by nearly eighty publications, including his 2009 papers in *Science* and *Nature* as well as his textbook *Science into Policy: Global Lessons from Antarctica* (Academic Press, 2002) and his co-edited book *Science Diplomacy: Antarctica, Science and the Governance of International Spaces* (Smithsonian Institution Scholarly Press, forthcoming). He was chair of the international board for the Antarctic Treaty Summit that was convened at the Smithsonian Institution on the treaty's fiftieth anniversary in 2009. He is also co-director of the NATO Advanced Research Workshop on Environmental Security in the Arctic Ocean that will be convened at the University of Cambridge in October 2010. Professor Berkman also serves as the chief executive officer of EvREsearch LTD, and as a director for the Foundation for the Good Governance of International Spaces.

Acknowledgements

I thank the Royal United Services Institute for inviting me to write this *Whitehall Paper*. I further thank colleagues and collaborators who have provided thoughtful comments on this paper at various stages: Adele Airoldi, John Ash, Malcolm Chalmers, William Eucker, Tobias Feakin, Shiloh Fetzek, Alf Håkon Hoel, Adrian Johnson, Terence McNamee, James McQuaid, Sven-Roald Nystø, Tim Reilly, James Stavridis and Kenneth Yalowitz. I also thank the many people who have kindly shared their insights about the Arctic Ocean, especially the steering committee of the Arctic Ocean Geopolitics Programme: Robert Culshaw, William Nuttall, Julian Dowdeswell, Peter Prokosch, Diana Wallis and Oran Young. This *Whitehall Paper* has also benefited from the planning of the NATO Advanced Research Workshop on Environmental Security in the Arctic Ocean at the University of Cambridge in October 2010, and I thank my co-director, Alexander Vylegzhanin, along with our steering committee (Lloyd Axworthy, Robert Corell and Olav Schram Stokke). This paper is a contribution from the Arctic Ocean Geopolitics Programme at the Scott Polar Research Institute and Judge Business School at the University of Cambridge.

Acronyms and Abbreviations

ACAP	Arctic Contaminants Action Program (Arctic Council)
AHDR	Arctic Human Development Report
AMAP	Arctic Monitoring and Assessment Program (Arctic Council)
AMEC	Arctic Military Environmental Co-operation
AMSA	Arctic Marine Shipping Assessment
ATS	Antarctic Treaty System
CAFF	Conservation of Arctic Fauna and Flora (Arctic Council)
DEW	Distance Early Warning
EEZ	Exclusive Economic Zone
EPPR	Emergency Prevention, Preparedness and Response (Arctic Council)
EU	European Union
IASC	International Arctic Science Committee
IGY	International Geophysical Year
IMO	International Maritime Organisation
IPCC	Intergovernmental Panel on Climate Change
IPY	International Polar Year
MARPOL	Convention on the Prevention of Pollution by Ships
NATO	North Atlantic Treaty Organisation
NEAFC	Convention on Future Multilateral Cooperation in North-East Atlantic Fisheries
OSCE	Organisation for Security and Cooperation in Europe
OSPAR	Convention for the Protection of the Marine Environment of the North-East Atlantic
PAME	Protection of the Arctic Marine Environment (Arctic Council)
ppt	parts salt per thousand parts water
SCAR	Scientific Committee on Antarctic Research
SDWG	Sustainable Development Working Group (Arctic Council)
SLBM	Submarine-Launched Ballistic Missile
START I	Treaty on the Reduction and Limitation of Strategic Offensive Arms
UK	United Kingdom of Great Britain and Northern Ireland
UN	United Nations
UNCLOS	United Nations Convention on the Law of the Sea
UNDP	United Nations Development Programme
UNECE	United Nations Economic Commission for Europe
UNEP	United Nations Environmental Programme
USA	United States of America
USSR	Union of Soviet Socialist Republics

FOREWORD

Like the lines of longitude intersecting at the North Pole, several important security challenges with environmental, political, human and energy dimensions also conjoin in the Arctic Ocean. Scientific consensus points to an Arctic region with retreating sea ice, melting land-mass ice sheets and thawing permafrost. It is no coincidence that our strategic interest in the Arctic warms with its climate. The time has come to think creatively of how to deal with the resulting changes, because common efforts and common destiny require common responsibility.

In this realm there are more questions than answers. What are the best entities and best mechanisms for resolving issues related to the changing conditions in the north: national governments, international governmental organisations, non-governmental organisations, multilateral agreements and treaties, or other instruments? What role should militaries play in the region? Upon what legal basis should territorial claims be adjudicated? What role should commerce have in the region?

This *Whitehall Paper* is important because it highlights the need to stimulate the debate now, through diverse channels and entities, to ensure that an appropriate and informed result ensues – one which balances the interest of territorial integrity, sovereignty, commerce, access and preservation. This paper defines the core issues and calls upon nations to come to consensus through co-operation and mutual understanding, because faltering at a critical time could possibly lead to conflict in the region.

As the polar ice cap melts, it creates opportunities for trade and commerce via new routes, allows access to untapped natural resources, and offers the promise of rich scientific and technological discovery and innovation.

These changes come with a price tag. That price is a collective imperative to manage the changes responsibly and comprehensively with regard to our global community's mutual interests in the region. In essence, the melting of the polar ice cap is a global concern because it has the potential to alter the geopolitical balance in the Arctic heretofore frozen in time.

The cascading interests and broad implications stemming from the effects of climate change should cause today's global leaders to pause, take stock, and unify their efforts to ensure the Arctic remains a zone of co-operation – rather than proceed down the icy slope towards a zone of competition, or worse, a zone of conflict. For that reason, now is the time to redouble our efforts to ensure there is a spirit of co-operation among nations to chart a determined path through the complex issues in the high north.

These significant environmental changes directly affect the Arctic Ocean region and its five coastal nations – Canada, Denmark/Greenland, Norway, the Russian Federation, and the United States. But the effects also indirectly reach well beyond the Arctic Circle to most nations of the world. The Arctic Ocean, like all oceans, therefore serves as a canvas for human interaction without the burden of geopolitical boundaries. This phenomenon invites the global community to establish dialogue and together forge paths to future success – unilateral action rarely succeeds in today's world.

When working through the complex social, political, legal, environmental and military topics associated with the Arctic, it is worthwhile turning to history for ideas on how best to solve our challenges. A great deal of intellectual and political capital went into establishing Antarctica as a peaceful region for the benefit of humankind. The peaceful use of Antarctica endures to this day as a model of purpose-driven international co-operation.

A series of protocols specifies rules for the proper development of Antarctica – many of those bedrock ideas can, and should, be carried north to the Arctic as the network of actors continues to establish their paths for dialogue.

But we must also be mindful that the geostrategic situation in the Arctic is not identical to the Antarctic. For instance, the southern pole does not have nations with territorial claims ringing the region. For now, the disputes in the north have been dealt with peacefully, but climate change could alter the equilibrium over the coming years in the face of temptation for exploitation of more readily accessible natural resources.

Therefore, the international community must go beyond the lessons learnt in the south. We should avoid the trap of mirroring the Antarctic when building the construct for the high north, because the context is different. But we should consider the Antarctic as proof positive of the possibilities inherent in international co-operation. The future of the Arctic Ocean may be constructed with the balance tipped more towards pragmatism then idealism, but which still remains firmly underpinned by the desire to keep peace and co-operation at the forefront.

Some may argue the Arctic should be completely free of military forces in order to preserve the goal of peace and universal utility to humankind, but I personally believe that the military has a rightful and necessary role in the high north. Not all military capabilities are designed for force. Rather, the totality of today's military forces represents a broad range of capability that has utility for an even broader spectrum of use. For instance, as more commercial entities, eco-tourists and others operate or travel through the Arctic Ocean, the likelihood of mishaps, hazards to navigation, or encroachment on sovereignty may require a military response.

The Arctic is an unforgiving environment for any type of operation, regardless of its purpose: commercial, civil, private or military. In all cases, it takes specialised knowledge and equipment to conduct business under these punishing conditions. The military has equipment and trained personnel that can operate, survive and facilitate access to this harsh environment.

We need a comprehensive approach, involving commercial, civil, private and military interaction and co-operation, to innovatively contend with intersecting security challenges in the region – there is a big difference between military assistance and militarisation. Ultimately, peaceful activities in the Arctic Ocean are something that will not be achieved by military means alone, but by the collective co-operation of our civilian leaders and their partners across the fabric of our societies.

Civilian government agencies, non-governmental organisations, think tanks, academic institutions and public-private enterprises complemented by military capability together form the basis of the comprehensive approach to security. A 'whole of society' response can resolve troublesome issues before they become problems. It is this effective balance of the civil-military relationship, or 'smart power', that will help avoid future conflict in the Arctic.

There is also an innovation quotient to comprehensive security. Innovation comes in many different forms: technologies, ideas, business practices and many others. Governments have a large responsibility to provide mechanisms and innovations for securing our interests. In order to do so they must harness assistance from all sectors of the society.

First and foremost, in dealing with the challenges of an uncertain future, institutions must develop meaningful policies, design and build innovative technologies, and otherwise inform the debate in order to build the 'needs-technology-policy' bridge. Appropriate organisations must be active and responsive to changing needs and build on long-term professional relationships characterised by co-operative sharing of requirements, ideas and technologies.

There are nations with vested interests already defined by geography and international law, and respected by the international community, which should be the basis for future conventions, appropriately tailored to the future, but deeply-rooted in the success of the past.

The most prominent of those is the United Nations Convention on the Law of the Sea (UNCLOS). This landmark convention established a well-recognised legal system for determining the sovereign rights of nations as they pertain to the sea. Although the UNCLOS has not been ratified by the United States, it is observed in principle by that country.

Organisations also play a critical role in the process. In the case of the Arctic region, the Arctic Council and its six subcommittees provide a good and necessary forum for propelling the dialogue and achieving tangible results beneficial to the cause. The ideas generated in organisations that share mutual interests must be transferred to governments and formalised as treaties, conventions, or other binding instruments.

For example, although the United States and Russia have divergent interests at times, the two former Cold War adversaries can benefit from deliberately embarking on a campaign to find areas of common interest in the Arctic. Although military engagement is one form of co-operation and can serve as a foundation for broader co-operation, there are many other topics where the two nations may share interests.

Defining areas of common interest is the first step to enhanced co-operation, especially in the fields of scientific exploration and technological development. Increased co-operation in this arena naturally leads to better and more advanced technology, which generally has spin-offs across a wide swath of international society. Other areas of potential dialogue might also include the effects of global warming, navigation, pollution prevention and effects mitigation, search and rescue, environmental stewardship and fisheries.

This concept is very much analogous to the co-operative spirit which exists between the US and Russia (and other nations) in manned space flight. The Mir space station has been a remarkable project because it has brought participants closer together and fostered cultural understanding between nations. Better cultural understanding brings down barriers to trust, which in turn allows progress and in many cases increased security.

The work contained herein is thought provoking and worthy of consideration in the context of debating how to build a foundation that strengthens multinational co-operation beneficial to the future of the high north. This paper contains ample detail regarding the various legal and policy stances which frame the current – but dynamic – situation in the region. It is packed with detailed information regarding myriad organisations and treaties that contribute to the body of knowledge about the region. It also makes important links between other concepts, laws and treaties that are applicable to the high north. Readers will clearly see the depth of research and the importance of moving forward in determined fashion toward common and peaceful purpose.

The Arctic is vitally important to our globalised international community and, therefore, must receive our informed and collective attention over the near term. We must ensure our efforts provide a stabilising element that keeps the Arctic accessible for the lawful use of all nations, and those efforts must be built on a solid footing reinforced by co-operation and collective resolve.

James G Stavridis
Admiral, US Navy

1. INTRODUCTION

Within our lifetime, the Arctic Ocean will transform from a permanent sea-ice cap to a seasonally ice-free sea. Like a fertile area becoming a desert or a glacier becoming a mountain valley, this is an environmental state-change where the boundary conditions and dynamics of the system are fundamentally replaced.[1] Consider that the boundaries of the Arctic Ocean have been the sea-ice cap, the sea floor and surrounding continents, with inflow-outflow from the North Pacific and North Atlantic, together with solar forcing from the Sun. Removing the sea-ice cap fundamentally alters the dynamics of this Arctic Ocean system. Over timescales that are relevant to humans in the region, even in a historical context over centuries and millennia, the new Arctic Ocean is unprecedented.

Consequences of the environmental state-change in the Arctic Ocean are explored in this paper, with focus on the overlying geopolitical risks that will influence sustainable development across the maritime region at the top of the Earth. These risks are characterised in terms of political, economic and cultural instabilities that are herein defined as events or operations requiring governments to allocate resources in an unplanned manner, or at the expense of previously prioritised activities. These resources could be financial, diplomatic or intellectual, as well as tangible assets that are relevant to the security and welfare of the governments and the human populations that they represent.

The first objective of this paper is to introduce environmental security as a holistic framework to address the inherent risks of political, economic and cultural instabilities that

---

[1] M Scheffer, S Carpenter, J A Foley, C Folkes and B Walker, 'Catastrophic shifts in ecosystems', *Nature* (No. 413, 2001), pp. 591–96.

are emerging as the Arctic Ocean is transformed into a new natural system. In the absence of a holistic approach, it is likely that a patchwork of institutions will emerge, leading to a fragmented approach to governance. Environmental security is defined herein as an integrated approach for assessing and responding to the risks, as well as the opportunities, generated by environmental state-change.

This definition of environmental security is without reference to the cause of the environmental state-change, which could be related to indirect impacts of the Earth's climate or direct impacts from specific human activities, such as pollution or armed conflict.[2] Responses to environmental security involve regional, international and global considerations with co-ordinated responses.[3]

Future engagement will be required to assess and agree on the common risks (which are beyond the scope of this *Whitehall Paper*). Such risk assessment is the first step toward identifying the necessary adaptation and mitigation responses, which will enable human activities to mature with stability in the Arctic Ocean. With a shared understanding about the necessary infrastructure, it then becomes feasible to determine whether existing institutions are adequate within the international legal framework of the law of the sea. Consequently, it is argued that broad governance discussions are currently premature without a holistic vetting of the risks as well as a common understanding of the integrated responses for human development to be sustained in the Arctic Ocean.[4]

---

[2] American Council for the United Nations University, Millennium Project on Environmental Security Studies, <http://millenium-project.org/millenium/env-sec1.html>.

[3] K M Lietzman, and G D Vest, 'Environment and Security in an International Context', *Environmental Change and Security Report* (No. 5, 1999), pp. 34–68, <http://www.wilsoncenter.org/topics/pubs/Report5-Sect2-a.pdf>.

[4] P A Berkman, 'Integrated Arctic Ocean Governance for the Lasting Benefit of All Humanity' in G Witschel, I Winkelmann, K Tiroch and R Wolfrum (eds), *New Chances and New Responsibilities in the Arctic Region* (Berlin: Berliner Wissencshcafts-Verlag, 2009), pp. 187–94.

Rather than trying to conceive detailed recommendations, this paper is simply designed to establish a pathway for addressing security matters in the Arctic Ocean in an international, interdisciplinary and inclusive manner. This is intended for consideration by policy-makers who have the overriding responsibility to promote co-operation and prevent conflict in the Arctic Ocean, both in their own interests and for the common good.

Moving Beyond the Cold War: Peace as an Arctic Consideration

The challenges today are no different to those during the Cold War, as described by President Gorbachev in his seminal 1987 Murmansk speech:[5]

> The potential of contemporary civilization could permit us to make the Arctic habitable for the benefit of the national economies and other human interests of the near-Arctic states, for Europe and the entire international community. To achieve this, security problems that have accumulated in the area should be resolved above all.

These security problems are broader than just military issues, illustrated by the ongoing strategic deployment of nuclear submarines with ballistic missiles.

After the end of the Cold War, the Arctic states and indigenous peoples collectively established sustainable development as a common interest. In this new era, co-operation has flourished, especially with the high-level forum of the Arctic Council. Tensions have been low, even with the strategic military activities which have been ongoing in the Arctic Ocean for the past half-century. Territorial disputes are being dealt with in an amicable fashion. Everything appears to be going along smoothly. The environmental state-change in the Arctic

---

[5] Mikhail Gorbachev, speech in Murmansk at the Ceremonial Meeting on the Occasion of the Presentation of the Order of Lenin and the Gold Star to the City of Murmansk, 1 October 1987. English translation prepared by the Press Office of the Soviet Embassy, Ottawa, 1988, <http://www.barentsinfo.fi/docs/Gorbachev_speech.pdf>.

Ocean, however, is a game-changer and it is therefore imprudent to be complacent.

The Arctic Council's progress illustrates the challenges in responding to the consequences of a new Arctic Ocean. With its establishment in 1996,[6] the Arctic Council began 'to provide a means for promoting cooperation ... on common arctic issues,* in particular issues of sustainable development and environmental protection'. The asterisk (which is included in the quote) is shorthand for 'the Arctic Council should not deal with matters related to military security', which means that strategies to prevent conflict have been avoided. Moreover, because it was equated with demilitarisation, 'peace' was specifically excluded from the 1996 Ottawa Declaration that established the Arctic Council. This Cold War posture continues, as demonstrated by the five Arctic coastal states in their 2008 Ilulissat Declaration, in which they discuss their 'stewardship role', but make no mention of peace or stability in the Arctic Ocean.

Though the Arctic Council (in collaboration with partner organisations, such as the International Arctic Science Committee) has produced many meaningful reports, the absence of the military dimensions of the Arctic have compromised its ability to consider holistic solutions. This dilemma is illustrated by the 2009 Arctic Marine Shipping Assessment (AMSA), which is the most comprehensive analysis of Arctic shipping ever produced. Even though coastguards have a necessary role in emergency responses for pollution prevention and clean-up as well as safety-of-life at sea, 'in keeping with the scope of the Arctic Council, naval or military vessels were not included in the AMSA database'.

With the opening of trade routes across the Arctic Ocean from the North Atlantic to the North Pacific, trillion-dollar business opportunities will alter the global balance of power – as other new trade routes have before them. Dismissing the peaceful use of military assets in support of global trade and commercial activities in the Arctic Ocean, just because the region involves strategic deployments, is an unnecessary Cold War-era complication.

---

[6] Declaration on the Establishment of the Arctic Council, Ottawa, 19 September 1996. <http://www.international.gc.ca/polar-polaire/ottdec-decott.aspx>.

Environmental security is a strategy to unblock this loggerhead and enable appropriate military assets to be considered in building the capacity for sustainable development in the new Arctic Ocean. An indication of post-Cold War progress would be for the Arctic coastal states, including the United States and Russian Federation, to explicitly identify peace in the Arctic Ocean as another common Arctic issue.

The Environmental Security Framework

The second objective of this paper is to establish environmental security as a framework for shared dialogue to both promote co-operation and prevent conflict in the Arctic Ocean: two sides of the coin of peace. One outcome of these dialogues will be strategies that balance national and common interests in the Arctic Ocean, establishing precedents for human activities across and beyond sovereign jurisdictions elsewhere in the world.

This paper is organised into four chapters, followed by a concluding segment. Concepts and details in the chapters are embedded within three subsections to reduce the complexity of the diverse elements associated with environmental security in the Arctic Ocean. Figures and tables are used to further synthesise the information and highlight key arguments. In addition, primary resources are referenced, rather than media digests, to enhance the rigour of the analyses and to facilitate additional assessments by the reader.

Chapter 2 (The Arctic Ocean) introduces the spatial and temporal dimensions of an environmental security approach by describing the geography, characteristics and dynamics of this marine region that is surrounded by continents and centred over the North Pole. The Arctic and the Arctic Ocean have many definitions.[7] For the purposes of this paper, as well as for

---

[7] Various definitions of the Arctic can be found in A H Hoel, 'The High North Legal-Political Regime' in S G Holtsmark and B A Smith-Windsor (eds), *Security Prospects in the High North: Geostrategic Thaw or Freeze?* (Rome: NATO Defense College, 2009), pp. 81–101. Definitions of the Arctic also have been mapped by the United Nations Environment Programme (UNEP), GRID Arendal, <http://maps.grida.no/go/graphic/definitions_of_the_arctic>.

management strategies based on a geographic setting that can be consistently compared over time, the Arctic Ocean is defined herein as the marine region north of the Arctic Circle (66.5° north latitude). The human dimensions of the Arctic Ocean are presented here largely in the context of the indigenous peoples who have inhabited this region for millennia.

The long-standing boundary conditions of the Arctic Ocean as a natural system, with the sea floor and persistent sea-ice cap surrounded by continents, are also discussed. Satellite and submarine datasets from above and below the sea ice, respectively, demonstrate the decreasing horizontal and vertical dimensions of the sea-ice cap over the past few decades. Results from independent models further indicate that the Arctic Ocean will be seasonally ice-free with open water across the North Pole – an environmental state-change that is replacing the surface boundary condition and fundamentally transforming the Arctic Ocean into a new natural system – by the middle of this century.

Chapter 3 (Beyond National Boundaries) expands on the Arctic Ocean environmental state-change in the context of Earth system processes and international frameworks operating beyond the scope of individual nations. Societal perspectives on climate are illustrated by the First International Polar Year in 1882–83, when European nations began to recognise that their agriculture and economies are directly impacted by global changes taking place across decades and centuries. The internal dynamics of the Arctic marine ecosystem further illustrate the fluid nature of the ocean and atmosphere, independent of sovereign jurisdictions.

The interconnectedness of our natural world extends to our civilisation, recognising that we inexorably became a global society during the twentieth century, as illustrated by two world wars and the steep growth of international legal frameworks in the aftermath. The chapter also explores the diverse engagement of both Arctic and non-Arctic states in the high north, to underscore the reality of broad international interest, capacity and responsibilities for decision-making with regard to Arctic Ocean affairs. Such international engagement is further justified by the emergence during the second half of the twentieth century of legal frameworks for international spaces that exist beyond sovereign jurisdictions.

In view of its transboundary and international dimensions, Chapter 4 (Matters of Security) broadly investigates the consequences of the Arctic Ocean environmental state-change in terms of geopolitical risks in the region. Political stability in and around the Arctic Ocean is considered since the end of the Cold War, largely following the 1987 Murmansk speech by President Gorbachev, who was extending lessons from the Antarctic to the Arctic. With the International Arctic Science Committee as an analogue to the Scientific Committee on Antarctic Research, scientific exploration has become both a diplomatic tool that promotes international co-operation and a research tool that contributes to basic assessments in the Arctic Ocean. Moreover, building on President Gorbachev's suggestion for an 'Arctic Research Council', the Arctic Council has established a meaningful presence as the high-level forum to address the common Arctic issues of sustainable development and environmental protection.

Differences between the Arctic and Antarctic, however, demonstrate that governance strategies are not portable, as shown by the 2008 Ilulissat Declaration[8] of the five Arctic coastal states who 'see no need to develop a new comprehensive international legal regime to govern the Arctic Ocean'. Among the most significant differences is the long-standing military presence in the Arctic Ocean, as demonstrated by the tests of submarine-launched ballistic missiles since 1961. Such activities have complicated the realisation of President Gorbachev's vision to 'let the North Pole be a pole of peace'.

Well before the environmental state-change in the Arctic Ocean was recognised, President Gorbachev suggested '[opening] the Northern Sea Route to foreign ships'. Clearly, significant economic opportunities are now on the horizon in the Arctic Ocean: from the exploitation of mineral and living resources to global trade and commerce. To plan effectively for the future in the

---

[8] The Ilulissat Declaration from the Arctic Ocean Conference, 28 May 2008, Ilulissat, Greenland. <http://www.oceanlato.org/downloads/arctic/Ilulissat_Declaration.pdf>.

Arctic Ocean, lessons must be learnt from far and wide. For example, mineral resource estimates on the Antarctic continental shelf in the wake of the 1973–74 oil embargo closely parallel the quantities of oil and gas that are estimated on the Arctic continental shelf today. Similarly, the opening of trade routes across the Arctic Ocean is analogous to the early twentieth century, when paved roads were being considered to accommodate the onslaught of motor vehicles that would be travelling across continents. Assessing the integrated risks of political, economic and cultural instabilities will lead to an understanding of the appropriate logistic and legal infrastructures needed to establish sustained stable development in the Arctic Ocean for the security of all stakeholders.

Chapter 5 (Arctic Ocean Stewardship) recognises that implementation of the appropriate infrastructure in the Arctic Ocean will involve the interplay of diverse institutions. Some of the institutions, including government agencies of the Arctic coastal states, will have more central roles than others. All of these institutions fall across a gradient of jurisdictions – from states to international spaces – within the international legal framework of the law of the sea, to which all of the Arctic coastal states 'remain committed', as they noted in the 2008 Ilulissat Declaration. From the perspectives of the sea floor and the overlying water column, the Arctic Ocean illustrates the challenge of balancing national interests and common interests.

The concluding chapter (Global Statesmanship) is as much a synthesis of the paper as a call for the requisite leadership to achieve peace and stability in the Arctic Ocean. Environmental security is a valuable commodity – 'Environment must also be an approach to development. Environment is a social justice issue and environment even is a peace and security issue'[9] – and hence is the focus of the paper. There is no room for complacency just because tensions have been low. The environmental

---

[9] World Commission on Environment and Development, 'Our Common Future: From One Earth to One World', report transmitted to the UN General Assembly as an annex to Resolution A/RES/42/187 (United Nations: Geneva, 1987).

state-change offers an opportunity to address the emergent political, economic and cultural instabilities in the Arctic Ocean through the concept of environmental security. The challenge is to facilitate dialogue that is international, interdisciplinary and inclusive, and which both promotes co-operation and prevents conflict in the Arctic Ocean for the lasting benefit of all.

2. THE ARCTIC OCEAN

The Arctic Ocean is centred over the North Pole at 90°N (Figure 1). It is an ocean basin surrounded by continents, unlike Antarctica, which is a continent surrounded by ocean.

Figure 1: *See colour plate on p. 21*

Arctic continental shelves are the shallowest and broadest in the world with widths over 1,500 km adjacent to Siberia (Figure 1). The adjacent deep-water areas are divided by three submarine ridges (Alpha, Lomonosov and Nansen-Gakkel) with the Canada, Makarov, Amundsen and Nansen basins in the adjacent deep-water areas. The Arctic Ocean is also connected to the world ocean circulation with its inflow-outflow through the North Atlantic and North Pacific.

The Arctic Ocean has been defined by the International Hydrographic Organization with specific latitude and longitude boundaries that are related to various seas, islands, capes, straits, passages and bays.[1] The seas associated with the Arctic Ocean include (from east to west): Bering Sea, East Siberian Sea, Laptev Sea, Kara Sea, Barents Sea, Norwegian Sea, Greenland Sea, Labrador Sea and Beaufort Sea. The Arctic Ocean is the smallest of the world's oceans (Table 1).

---

[1] International Hydrographic Organization, *Limits of Oceans and Seas*, 3rd edition (Monaco: Special Publications No. 2, 1953), <http://www.iho-ohi.net/iho_pubs/standard/S-23/S23_1953.pdf> and map <http://www.iho-ohi.net/iho_pubs/standard/S-23/S23_Ed3_Sheet_1_Small.jpg>.

Table 1: Comparison of the Earth's Five Oceans.

	Percentage of Earth's Surface	Size (million km^2)	Greatest Depth (m)	Average Depth (m)
Pacific	30.5	155.56	10,911	4,300
Atlantic	20.8	76.76	8,605	3,300
Indian	14.4	65.56	7,258	3,900
Southern	4.0	20.33	7,235	4,000–5,000
Arctic	2.8	14.06	5,160	1,050

Source: Protection of the Arctic Marine Environment (PAME), 'Arctic Marine Shipping Assessment Report 2009' (Trømso: Arctic Council, 2009).

Other definitions of the Arctic Ocean also exist. Most prominently, as demonstrated by the 2008 Ilulissat Declaration,[2] the five surrounding states (Canada, Denmark through Greenland and the Faroe Islands, Norway, the Russian Federation and the United States) together have defined the Arctic Ocean in terms of their coastal boundaries north of the Arctic Circle (which is approximately 66.5°N). Their collective definition ignores, however, the fact that Iceland has the tiny (less than 90 m^2 with an elevation of 8 m), eroding, basaltic island of Kolbeinsey just north of 67°N.

Individually, the Arctic coastal states also use different definitions of the Arctic Ocean. For example, in its definition of the Arctic, the United States includes the marine areas in the Chuckchi Sea and Aleutian Islands to the south of the Arctic Circle.[3] The application by the United States of its broader definition for the Arctic Ocean is reflected by the shipping data it provided for the 2009 Arctic Marine Shipping Assessment.[4] The challenge is to identify a mutually acceptable definition of the Arctic Ocean that can be applied consistently for operational decisions that will need to be made in the future.

---

[2] The Ilulissat Declaration from the Arctic Ocean Conference, 28 May 2008, Ilulissat, Greenland, <http://www.oceanlaw.org/downloads/arctic/Ilulissat_Declaration.pdf>.

[3] United States Government, Arctic Research and Policy Act of 1984 (amended 1990), <http://www.nsf.gov/od/opp/arctic/iarpc/arc_res_pol_act.jsp>.

[4] PAME, *op. cit.*

The Arctic Circle (like the Antarctic Circle at the other antipodes) is based on the tilt of the Earth's axis, which is approximately 23.5° off vertical. In the polar regions, the tilt of the Earth's axis affects the presence or absence of sunlight like a switch, controlling the dynamics of associated ecosystems as they progress from complete darkness to complete sunlight, twenty-four hours per day. Without the Earth's axial tilt, the season at each latitude would be unchanging throughout the year. This has relevance to the oceanography and ecology of the marine system.

An advantage of defining the boundary of the Arctic Ocean based on the Arctic Circle is that it provides a uniform circumpolar position, which can easily be identified by tools such as global positioning systems. For the purposes of this *Whitehall Paper*, **the Arctic Ocean is defined as the circumpolar marine region north of the Arctic Circle (66.5°N).**

Surrounded by People

The Arctic Ocean is part of the geopolitical context of the surrounding coastal states, as well as of Finland and Sweden, both of which have territory north of the Arctic Circle but lack a coastline on the Arctic Ocean. Together, the 'Arctic Eight' represent the sovereign jurisdictions in the north polar region (Table 2).

The Canadian Arctic Archipelago across the Northwest Territories and Nunavut contains ninety-four islands greater than 130 km^2, including the fifth, seventh and tenth largest islands in the world: Baffin Island (over 507,000 km^2), Victoria Island (over 217,000 km^2) and Ellesmere Island (over 196,000 km^2). The various major islands, along with more than 36,000 minor islands in the Canadian Arctic Archipelago, are separated from each other and the North American continent by a series of shallow-draft waterways that collectively represent the fabled Northwest Passage.

With a total land area exceeding 1,400,000 km^2, the Canadian Arctic Archipelago is the second largest land area in the Arctic Ocean next to Greenland (over 2,130,000 km^2), which is the world's largest island. Moving eastward is the Russian archipelago of Novaya Zemlya, which has two major and several smaller islands (total area over 90,000 km^2) along the Siberian

Table 2: Recognised Sovereignty of the Arctic Nation States.

Nation	History of Sovereignty[a] Date	Basis	UNCLOS Ratification[b]
Canada[c]	1 July 1867	British North America Act	7 November 2003
Denmark[c]	3 July 1721 14 January 1814	Colonisation of Greenland, Treaty of Kiel (Faroe Island)	16 November 2004
Finland	6 December 1917	Declaration of Independence from Russia	21 June 1996
Iceland	17 June 1944	Declaration of Independence from Denmark	21 June 1985
Norway[c]	18 November 1905 9 February 1920 8 May 1929	Dissolution of Dual Monarchy with Sweden, Spitsbergen Treaty, Annexation of Jan Mayen	24 June 1996
Sweden	6 June 1523	Accession of King Gustav Vasa	25 June 1996
Russia[c]	15 April 1926	Declaration of the Soviet Presidium	12 March 1997
United States[c]	30 March 1867	Purchase of Alaska from Russia	Not Yet Ratified[d]

Source: Adapted from: P A Berkman, 'Arctic Ocean State-Changes: Self Interests or Common Interests', in G Alfredsson, T Koivurova, and D K Leary (eds.), *Yearbook of Polar Law: Volume 1* (Leiden: Martinus Nijhoff Publishers, 2009), pp. 527–41.

a Sovereignty data in this table have been compiled by R K Headland.

b United Nations Convention on the Law of the Sea (UNCLOS), Montego Bay, Jamaica, 10 December 1982 with entry into force on 16 November 1994.

c Coastline north of the Arctic Circle (66.5°N).

d Even though they have not yet ratified UNCLOS (as of this publication), the United States does recognise the territorial sea, contiguous zone, exclusive economic zone, continental shelf, deep sea and high seas under customary international law.

continental shelf between the Barents and Kara Seas across northwest Russia.

Among the nearly 4 million human inhabitants in the Arctic region, in addition to the citizens of the Arctic coastal and non-coastal states, are the indigenous peoples who represent various percentages of the populations (Figure 2). The indigenous peoples have lived at the Arctic Ocean for tens of millennia.[5] In fact, the land bridge of Beringia enabled indigenous populations to walk between present-day Alaska and eastern Siberia during the Last Glacial Maximum, nearly 17,000 years ago.[6]

Figure 2: *See colour plate on p. 22*

There are more than forty languages grouped into at least seven language families, representing the cultural and social diversity of the Arctic as a region.[7] More than 130,000 humans inhabit the Canadian Arctic Archipelago, with Inuit representing more than half of the population. Greenland, which has self-government as part of Denmark,[8] has a population of more than 57,000 people, nearly 90 per cent of whom are Inuit or mixed Danish and Inuit. The northernmost region of Norway is the archipelago of Svalbard, encompassing an area of more than 61,000 km² with about 2,500 people on the islands of Spitsbergen, Longyearbyen and Hopen. Further eastwards, although officially Russia only recognises some 50,000 indigenous persons, it is estimated that there may be around 250,000 individuals in the Russian Arctic, ranging from large groups such as the Evenk and Nenets to small

---

[5] P Pavlov, J I Svendsen and S Indrelid, 'Human Presence in the European Arctic Nearly 40,000 Years Ago', *Nature* (Vol. 413, 2001), pp. 64–67; R McGhee, *The Last Imaginary Place: A Human History of the Arctic World* (Toronto: Key Porter Books/Canadian Museum of Civilization, 2004).

[6] T Goebel, M R Waters and D H O'Rourke, 'The Late Pleistocene Dispersal of Modern Humans in the Americas', *Science* (Vol. 319, No. 5869), pp. 1497–1502.

[7] Y Csonka and P Schweitzer, 'Societies and Cultures: Change and Persistence', in Larsen, *op. cit.*, pp. 45–68.

[8] Naalakkersuisut [Greenland Government] and Danish Government, *Act on Greenland Self-Government*, entry into force on 21 July 2009, <http://uk.nanoq.gl/~/media/f74bab3359074b29aab8c1e12aa1ecfe.ashx>.

groups such as the Enets and Orok.[9] In any case, the largest human presence in the Arctic exists in Russia, where most of the population is non-indigenous (Figure 2).

The Sámi peoples of Northern Europe, estimated to total around 100,000, are politically represented by three Sámi parliaments in Sweden, Norway and Finland. In 2000, these three Sámi parliaments established a council of representatives between them, called the Sámi Parliamentary Council. In Norway, the status of the Sámi as a people is officially recognised by a constitutional amendment. In contrast, Finland considers its approximately 7,000 Sámi to be a linguistic minority rather than an indigenous people.

The Inuit from Alaska, Canada, Russia and Greenland represent the largest indigenous presence in the Arctic region. In 1973, these populations formed the Inuit Circumpolar Council, which co-ordinated adoption of the Circumpolar Inuit Declaration on Arctic Sovereignty in April 2009.[10]

Starting with the Vikings from Iceland who settled with the Inuits in Greenland nearly a thousand years ago,[11] indigenous peoples of the high north have been progressively impacted by humans from outside of the region. **Nonetheless, the resilient presence of the indigenous peoples around the Arctic Ocean, through glacial and interglacial climate periods, reflects the long-term perspective that is required in adopting strategies that have a planetary scope**. There is much to learn from the indigenous knowledge of the Arctic peoples.

Environmental State-Change

The Arctic Ocean as a system is characterised by its boundary conditions, internal components and interactions with other

---

[9] United Nations Permanent Forum on Indigenous Issues, 'Indigenous Peoples in the Arctic Region Fact Sheet', <http://www.unis.unvienna.org/pdf/factsheets/Permanent_Forum_Indigenous_Issues_2009_factsheet2.pdf>.

[10] Circumpolar Declaration on Arctic Sovereignty, April 2009, <http://www.itk.ca/circumpolar-inuit-declaration-arctic-sovereignty>.

[11] W W Fitzhugh and E I Ward (eds), *Vikings: The North Atlantic Saga* (Washington, DC: Smithsonian Institute Press, 2000).

systems (including the North Pacific and North Atlantic as well as the atmosphere) with external forcing from the Sun. Changing any of the boundary conditions of the Arctic Ocean will effectively create a new system.

As a system, the boundaries of the Arctic Ocean historically have been the sea floor, surrounding continents and its year-round cover of sea ice. The Arctic Ocean is permanently covered, mostly by multi-year sea ice (in other words, older than two years).[12] Around Antarctica, by contrast, the Southern Ocean is covered by sea ice that expands and contracts from nearly 3 to 19 million km² each year.

Now, with the amplified impacts of climate warming in the polar regions,[13] a fundamental transformation in the boundary conditions of the Arctic Ocean is underway with the progressive loss of its sea-ice cover as indicated independently by data from below and above. Since the 1950s submarines have been transiting under the sea ice, taking upward-looking sonar measurements of sea-ice thickness. While actual paths of these submarines are mostly classified, sonar data have been released at a spatial scale that is sufficient to detect a clear trend of decreasing sea-ice thickness from a maximum of 3.4 m in 1980 to a minimum of 2.3 m in 2000 (Figure 3a). Downward-looking satellite data further indicate that the monthly May sea-ice extent in the Arctic Ocean has declined 2.5 per cent per decade from 1979 to 2009, an average of 43,000 km² decrease per year (Figure 3b). This trend indicates that the Arctic Ocean is becoming like the Southern Ocean surrounding Antarctica, with annual sea-ice growth and retreat across most of the ocean area.

---

[12] P Wadhams and J C Comiso, 'The Ice Thickness Distribution Inferred using Remote Sensing Techniques' in F Carsey (ed.), *Microwave Remote Sensing of Sea Ice* (Washington, DC: American Geophysical Union, 1992), pp. 375–83.

[13] S Manabe and R J Stouffer, 'Sensitivity of a Global Climate Model to an Increase of CO_2 Concentration in the Atmosphere', *Journal of Geophysical Research* (Vol. 85, 1980), pp. 5529–54; R E Moritz, C M Bitz and E J Steig, 'Dynamics of Recent Climate Change in the Arctic', *Science* (Vol. 297, 2002), pp. 1497–501.

Figure 3: Environmental state-change in the Arctic Ocean from a permanent sea-ice cap to a seasonally ice-free ocean revealed from independent types of analyses: **(a)** upward-looking submarine sonar data of the areally and annually averaged ice thickness (solid line) with superimposed annual cycle of 1 metre change in ice thickness;[14] **(b)** downward-looking satellite data of monthly May sea-ice extent in millions of km² showing the mean trend (solid line);[15] and **(c)** forecasts of sea-ice coverage from multiple National Center for Atmospheric Research models.[16]

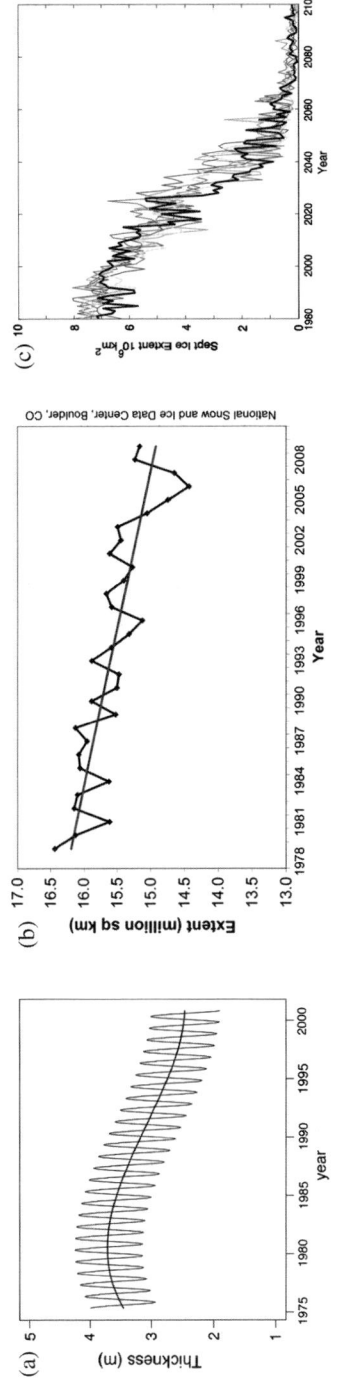

---

[14] D A Rothrock, D B Percival and M Wensnahan, 'The Decline in Arctic Sea-ice Thickness: Separating the Spatial, Annual, and Interannual Variability in a Quarter Century of Submarine Data', *Journal of Geophysical Research* (Vol. 113, 2008).
[15] National Snow and Ice Data Center, <http://nsidc.org/arcticseaicenews/2009/040609.html>.
[16] M M Holland, C M Bitz, and B Tremblay, 'Future Abrupt Reductions in the Summer Arctic Sea Ice', *Geophysical Research Letters*, L2350 (Vol. 33, 2006).

With climate as the external forcing,[17] models of the Arctic Ocean system indicate that the sea-ice cap will be absent during the boreal summer sometime in the mid-twenty-first century (Figure 3c), maybe as soon as within the next three decades.[18] Moreover, observations indicate that the downward trend in September Arctic sea-ice extent from 1953–2006 is faster than simulations from the Intergovernmental Panel on Climate Change (IPCC) and that current summer minima are approximately thirty years ahead of the IPCC forecast.[19]

Transformation from year-round sea-ice coverage to seasonally ice-free conditions during the boreal summer in the Arctic Ocean is unprecedented over at least the past 800,000 years.[20] This environmental state-change in the sea-ice boundary of the Arctic Ocean is abrupt, and neither gradual nor cyclic. The shift from one state to another is like fertile land transforming into a desert, or a glacial system disappearing into exposed mountain valleys. **In effect, a new Arctic Ocean system will emerge with different dynamics because of this environmental state-change.**

With diminished or absent sea-ice cover, the transfer of atmospheric heat into the Arctic Ocean will change, altering the formation of water masses in the high north[21] and their

---

[17] R G Barry, 'Arctic Ocean Ice and Climate: Perspectives on a Century of Polar Research', *Annals of the Association of American Geographers* (Vol. 73, 1983), pp. 485–501.

[18] M Wang and J E Overland, 'A Sea Ice Free Summer Arctic within 30 years?', *Geophysical Research Letters*, L07502 (Vol. 36, 2009).

[19] J Stroeve, M Marika, M M Holland, W Meier, T Scambos, and M Serreze, 'Arctic Sea Ice Decline: Faster than Forecast', *Geophysical Research Letters* (Vol. 34, 2007).

[20] J T Overpeck, M Sturm, J A Francis, D K Perovich, M C Serreze, R Benner, E C Carmack, F S Chapin III, S C Gerlach, L C Hamilton, L D Hinzman, M Holland, H P Huntington, J R Key, A H Lloyd, G M Macdonald, J McFadden, D Noone, T D Prowse, P Schlosser and C Vörösmarty, 'Arctic System on Trajectory to New, Seasonally Ice-Free State', *Transactions of the American Geophysical Union* (Vol. 86, No. 34, 2005), pp. 309–16.

[21] R Curry and C Mauritzen, 'Dilution of the Northern North Atlantic Ocean in Recent Decades', *Science* (Vol. 308, 2005), pp. 1772–73.

interaction with the global thermohaline circulation.[22] Albedo[23] will be reduced and, with less heat reflected back into space from the white sea-ice cover, there will be a positive feedback with global temperatures.

Winds blowing across the ocean surface will modify current patterns. Thinner or absent sea ice will enhance the penetration of light into the ocean, which will impact algal production and ultimately species at higher trophic levels throughout the food web. New species will enter into the Arctic marine ecosystem. Some of these changes will have impact on commercial fisheries, both in the water column and on the sea floor.

With open water, there will be increased wave action that will enhance erosion along Arctic coastlines, which in turn will impact dependent and associated human populations. Coastal erosion will also transfer sediments and any associated contaminants offshore.

Then, of course, there is the anticipated suite of commercial opportunities that will arise with reduced sea-ice coverage. There will be increased ship traffic: not only for fisheries, but for commercial transport of cargoes between the Pacific and the Atlantic that will alter global trade patterns. There also will be new access to offshore energy resources, which are hypothesised to be a significant percentage of the global supply of oil and gas.[24]

---

[22] Thermohaline circulation refers to the part of the large-scale ocean circulation that is driven by global density gradients created by surface heat and freshwater fluxes. The adjective thermohaline derives from 'thermo-' referring to temperature and '-haline' referring to salt content, factors which together determine the density of sea water. W S Broecker, 'Thermohaline Circulation, the Achilles Heel of our Climate System: Will Man-made CO_2 Upset the Current Balance?', *Science* (Vol. 78, No. 1, 1997), pp. 582–1,588.

[23] The albedo of an object is a measure of how strongly it reflects light from sources such as the Sun.

[24] D L Gautier, K J Bird, R R Charpentier, A Grantz, D W Houseknecht, T R Klett, T E Moore, J K Pitman, C J Schenk, J H Schuenemeyer, K Sørensen, M E Tennyson, Z C Valin and C J Wandrey, 'Assessment of Undiscovered Oil and Gas in the Arctic', *Science* (Vol. 324, 2009), pp. 1175–79.

These commercial opportunities will herald all manner of infrastructural changes, from the pending adoption of a binding polar code[25] to new ports and land-based facilities; circumpolar communication and monitoring systems; and emergency response networks that will involve commercial as well as military assets.[26] Along with the infrastructure changes, there will be associated legal, regulatory and administrative frameworks that operate at local, regional, national and international levels.[27] There may also be associated geo-engineering solutions to mitigate climate changes.[28]

Together, these impacts associated with the environmental state-change in the Arctic Ocean introduce risks of political, economic and cultural instabilities that are relevant to each of the Arctic states (see Table 2), individually and collectively. These instabilities, which compel governments to allocate resources with urgency in an unplanned manner, are also relevant to non-Arctic nations. The challenge is to both promote co-operation and prevent conflict with international, interdisciplinary and inclusive engagement to, first, assess the risks of instabilities; and second, establish the appropriate adaptation and mitigation responses.

---

[25] O Jensen, *The IMO Guidelines for Ships Operating in Arctic Ice-covered Waters From Voluntary to Mandatory Tool for Navigation Safety and Environmental Protection?* (Lysaker: Fridtjof Nansen Institute, 1995).

[26] Office of Naval Research, *Naval Operations in an Ice-Free Arctic: Symposium* (Annapolis: United States Naval Ice Center, 2001).

[27] L Brigham, 'The Fast-changing Maritime Arctic', *Proceedings of the US Naval Institute*, May 2010, pp. 54–59.

[28] B Egede-Nissen and H D Venema, 'Desperate Times, Desperate Measures: Advancing the Geoengineering Debate', Arctic Council International Institute for Sustainable Development, Manitoba, 2009, <http://www.iisd.org/pdf/2009/desperate_times_desperate_measures.pdf>.

The Arctic Ocean

Figure 1: International Bathymetric Chart of the Arctic Ocean.

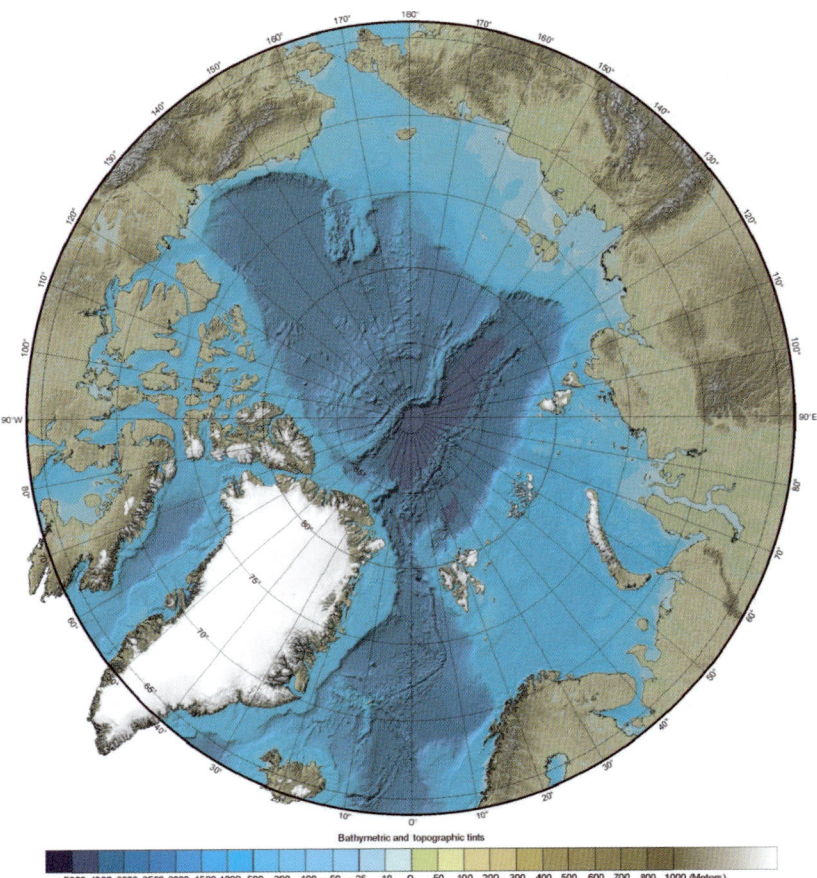

Note: Shows the physical system, ocean depths and terrestrial elevations in metres along with latitudes and longitudes to the North Pole, without geographic place names.

Environmental Security in the Arctic Ocean

Figure 2: Indigenous and Non-Indigenous Human Populations in the Arctic Region.

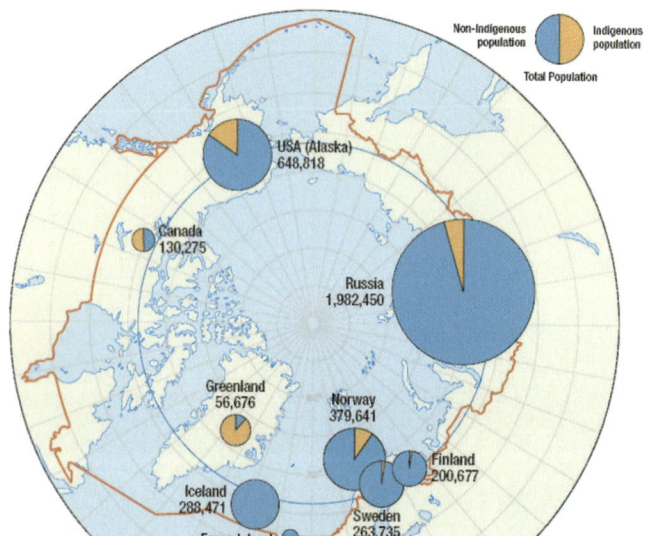

Note: Region encompasses more than 40 million km² across nearly 8 per cent of the Earth's surface, as defined by the Arctic Human Development Report (AHDR).

Figure 4a: The Mer de Glace Viewed from Montenvers, Mont Blanc Region, French Alps.

Note: The left-hand picture is an extract from an 1826 painting by Birman soon after the Little Ice Age maximum. The right-hand photograph was taken from a similar position in 2000. Arrows indicate similar positions on the glacier margins, and indicate the level of glacier-surface lowering.

Figure 5: Arctic Ocean Circulation.

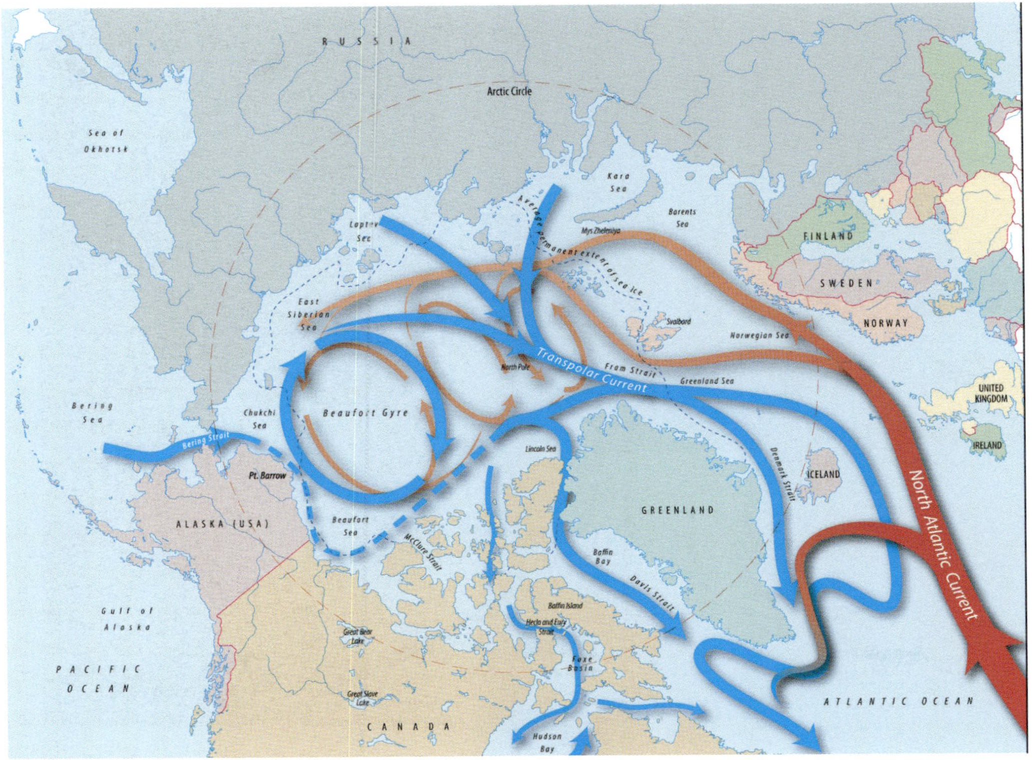

Note: Cold, relatively fresh seawater from the Pacific Ocean enters the through the Bering Strait before being swept into the Beaufort Gyre and exiting into the North Atlantic Ocean through the Fram, Davis, and Hudson Straits. Saltier, denser waters from the Atlantic Ocean enter the Arctic Ocean beneath the cold-water layers, which act as a barrier that reduces sea-ice melting.

Figure 6: Illustration of Interactions Among Species Associated with the Large Marine Ecosystem of the Arctic Ocean and its Various Sub-units.

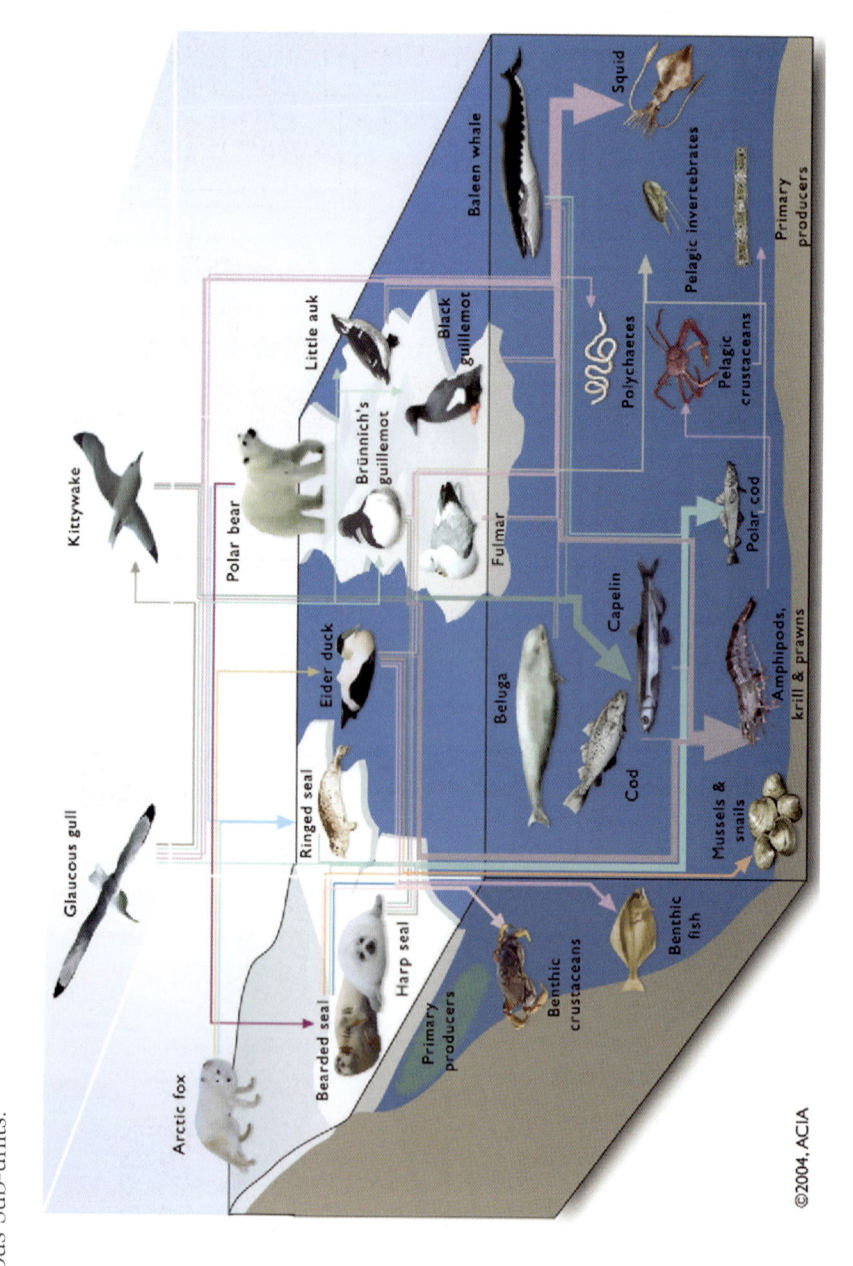

The Arctic Ocean

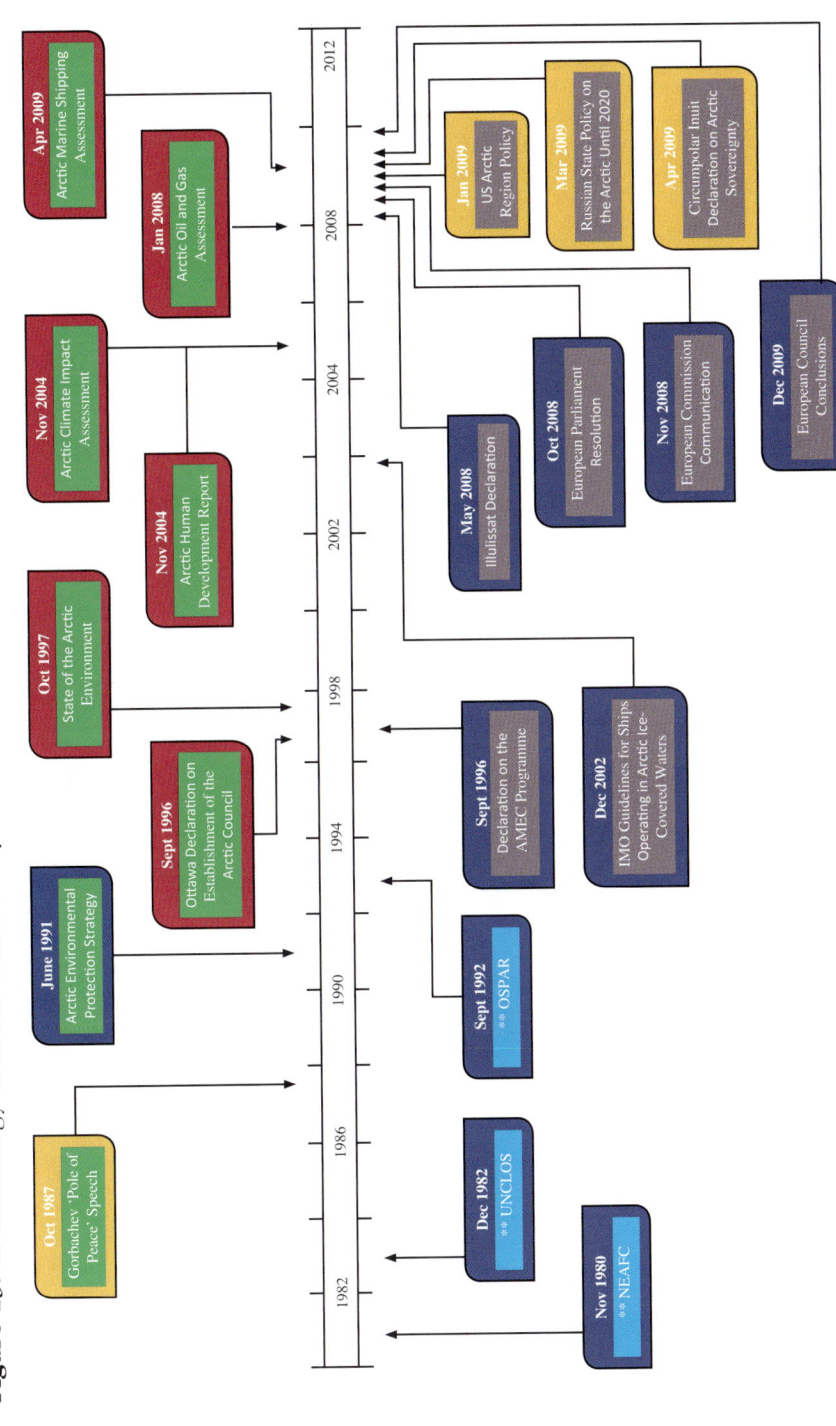

Figure 13: A Chronology of Arctic Ocean Policy Frameworks from End of Cold War to Present.

Environmental Security in the Arctic Ocean

Figure 14: Jurisdictional Representation of the Arctic Ocean, Seafloor Boundaries.

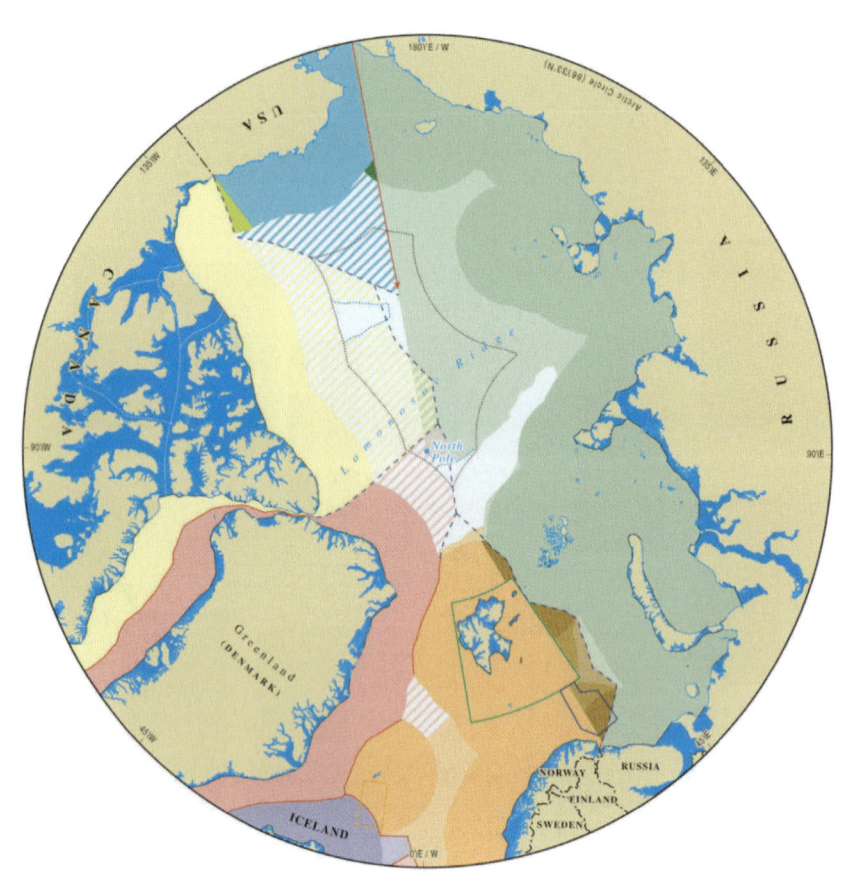

Note: Figure emphasises boundaries based on the seafloor – as a potential source of conflict among nations – with sovereign areas and outer continental shelf claims (different colours). See alternative jurisdictional representation of the Arctic Ocean based on the overlying water column (Figure 15).

Figure 15: Jurisdictional Representation of the Arctic Ocean, Water Column Boundaries.

Note: Figure emphasises boundaries based on the overlying water column – as a source of co-operation among nations – with the High Seas (dark blue) as an unambiguous international space in the central Arctic Ocean surrounded by Exclusive Economic Zones (light blue). See alternative jurisdictional representation of the Arctic Ocean based on the sea floor (Figure 14).

Figure References

Figure 1: M Jakobsson, R Macnab, L Mayer, R Anderson, M Edwards, J Hatzky, H W Schenke and P Johnson, 'An improved bathymetric portrayal of the Arctic Ocean: Implications for ocean modeling and geological, geophysical and oceanographic analyses', L07602, *Geophysical Research Letters* (Vol. 35, 2008). The high-resolution map, with information about its production, can be found at <http://www.ngdc.noaa.gov/mgg/bathymetry/arctic/arctic.html>.

Figure 2: O R Young and N Einarsson, 'Introduction' in J N Larsen (ed.), *Arctic Human Development Report, Sustainable Development Working Group, Arctic Council* (Akureyri: Stephanson Arctic Institute, 2004), pp. 15–26. <http://www.svs.is/AHDR/AHDR%20chapters/English%20version/AHDR_chp%201.pdf>.

Figure 4a: Painting from Gugelmann Collection, Swiss National Library, Bern; photo by M J Hambrey, 2000. <http://www.swisseduc.ch/glaciers/glossary/little-ice-age-two-en.html>.

Figure 5: L Lippsett, 'Is global warming changing the Arctic?', *Oceanus* (Vol. 44, No. 3, 2006), pp. 24–25.

Figure 6: AMAP, *Arctic Climate Impact Assessment* (Cambridge: Cambridge University Press, 2004). Interacting sub-units in the Large Marine Ecosystem of the Arctic Ocean (clockwise): East Bering Sea; West Bering Sea; Sea of Okhotsk; Chukchi Sea; East Siberian Sea; Laptev Sea; Kara Sea; Barents Sea; Norwegian Sea; Iceland Shelf Sea; East Greenland Shelf-Sea; West Greenland Shelf; Baffin Bay-Davis Strait; Hudson Bay; Canadian Arctic Archipelago; Beaufort Sea; and Central Arctic Ocean, <http://arcticportal.org/en/pame/ecosystem-approche>.

Figures 14 and 15: From P A Berkman and O R Young, 'Governance and environmental change in the Arctic Ocean', *Science* (No. 324, 2009), pp. 339–40. The original maps, which also include the legend of colours and features, are reproduced with permission from the International Boundaries Research Unit, University of Durham. The high-resolution version of Figure 14, which includes the legend of colours and features, can be found at the International Boundaries Research Unit, University of Durham, <http://www.dur.ac.uk/resources/ibru/arctic.pdf>.

3. BEYOND NATIONAL BOUNDARIES

Earth System Processes

In November 2008, the European Commission issued a communication about the Arctic stating that 'the European Union is inextricably linked to the Arctic region'.[1] Portrayed in art and literature (see Figure 4a), this has been known as far back as the nineteenth century. A prominent example of European interdependence with the Arctic is illustrated by the Little Ice Age. As the name implies, this period had pronounced cooling from 1150 to 1460, with very cold winters between 1560 and 1850. This centuries-long cold-weather pattern influenced agriculture, health, social dynamics and economies across Europe (Figure 4b).

Figure 4a: *See colour plate on p. 22*

When the Little Ice Age finally ended, scientific observations concluded that the persistent cold weather originated from the polar region. The period had brought economic and cultural shocks, such as food insecurity and high crop costs (Figure 4b), leading to initiation of the First International Polar Year (IPY) by European nations in 1882–83.[2] Responding to these significant security issues posed by climatic changes, in effect, the First IPY was the original international co-ordinated climate research programme.

---

[1] *European Commission Communication on the European Union and the Arctic Region* (Brussels: European Union, 2008), <http://ec.europa.eu/external_relations/arctic_region/docs/com_08_763_en.pdf>.
[2] P A Berkman, 'International Polar Year 2007–08', *Science* (Vol. 301, 2003), p. 1669.

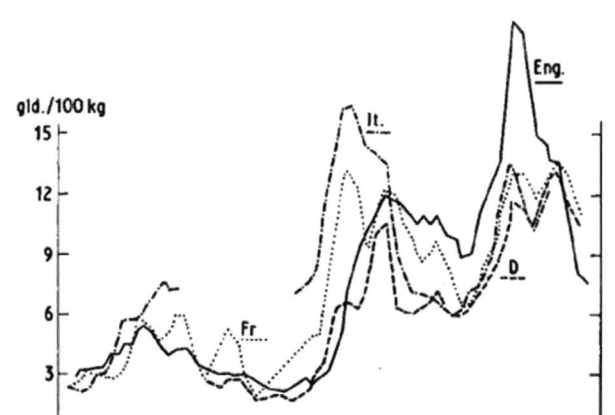

Figure 4b: Prices of Wheat Expressed in Dutch Guilders per 100 kg of Wheat in Italy, England, France Holland and Italy.[3]

Building on the experience, insights and lessons of the last 125 years, the international community convened the Fourth IPY from 2007–09.[4] The world has been developing strategies and technologies that enable us to peer into the future with constantly improving clarity. We are continuing to learn about the dynamics of the Earth system and its climate, which is a planetary process that integrates land, ocean, atmosphere and biota with system forcing from the Sun.

Unlike weather, which is regional with changes over seasons to years, climate changes are planetary, changing over decades to centuries. This distinction is an affront to short-term perspectives and 'business as usual'. Global society is going through growing pains to establish commensurate strategies and decade/century responses to the climate changes that we are forecasting with increasing reliability.

The environmental state-change in the Arctic Ocean from a permanent sea-ice cap to a seasonally ice-free sea (Figure 3) is among the most profound climate impacts on Earth today. The

---

[3] H H Lamb, *Climate, History and the Modern World* (London: Methuen, 1995).

[4] The 4th International Polar Year was convened from 1 March 2007–1 March 2009, <http://www.ipy.org>.

point here is not to assess the regional climate impacts, as is being accomplished with broad international and interdisciplinary collaboration through the Intergovernmental Panel on Climate Change,[5] but merely to illustrate the transboundary dimensions of the Arctic Ocean as an integral part of the Earth system.

Under the sea in the Arctic Ocean (Figure 5), currents and water masses circulate heat and salt (a process known as thermohaline circulation) as well as sea-ice, biological species, chemical elements and man-made pollutants throughout the basin (Figure 1). The Bering Strait connects the Arctic Ocean to the Pacific Ocean while the Greenland Sea, across the Faeroe-Icelandic Ridge, is the main conduit to the Atlantic Ocean. **As with any hydrographic system, water in the Arctic Ocean circulates across regions independently of human-imposed geopolitical boundaries**.

Figure 5: *See colour plate on p. 23*

In the Arctic Ocean, temperatures range from the freezing point of seawater (around −1.8°C, depending on salinity) at the surface, to a maximum around +2°C in the thermocline[6] at about 200 metres depth to −1.0°C at about 1,500 metres depth. Surface salinities range from 28–35 ppt (parts salt per thousand parts water) offshore, with much lower salinities in coastal areas where there is glacial runoff. With increased melting of glaciers due to climate warming – especially from Greenland, which has enough water locked in the ice to raise global sea level 6 to 7 metres[7] – salinities in coastal areas will be further diluted.

---

[5] Intergovernmental Panel on Climate Change, 'Climate Change 2007: Synthesis Report – A Summary for Policymakers', Fourth Assessment Report, November 2007, <www.ipcc.ch/pdf/assessment-report/ar4/syr/ar4_syr_spm.pdf>.

[6] This is the depth at which the rate of decrease of temperature with the increase of depth is the largest. It is a separation zone between the mixed-layer above, much influenced by atmospheric fluxes, and the deep ocean. The thermocline depth differs depending on geographical location, and can also have annual variations.

[7] K M Cuffey and S J Marshall, 'Substantial Contribution to Sea-level Rise during the Last Interglacial from the Greenland Ice Sheet', *Nature* (Vol. 404, 2000), pp. 591–94.

A significant outcome of the currents, temperatures, salinities, bathymetries[8] and meteorological synergy in the Arctic Ocean is its sea-ice. Historically, the Arctic Ocean has been covered predominantly by multi-year sea ice (Figure 3a), which is influenced by relatively fresh Pacific inflow into the shallow Laptev Sea, which serves as the 'ice factory of the Arctic Ocean'[9] (Figure 5). Consequently, currents associated with the North Pacific and North Atlantic, as well as temperature, salinity and meteorological conditions associated with the Arctic Ocean, all influence the extent of sea-ice coverage around the North Pole.

With the sinking of North Atlantic Deep Water into the deep sea, the Arctic Ocean also is connected to the 'global conveyor belt'[10] that distributes heat, salt and chemical elements throughout the world ocean. Consequently, transformation of the sea-ice coverage in the Arctic Ocean[11] and its associated parameters will lead to substantial changes in the global thermohaline circulation and density layering of the world ocean.[12]

During the polar summers in the Arctic and Antarctic, ice as a white body reflects most of the incoming solar radiation back into space, in contrast to water that absorbs nearly all of the solar radiation.[13] This ocean-ice-albedo feedback is a significant component of the global heat budget and it has been determined, as far back as the 1960s, that 'removing the Arctic sea-ice cap would increase annual average polar temperatures'

---

[8] Studies of the underwater depth of the ocean floor, the water equivalent of a topographic map that shows the relief and height of land features.
[9] M C Serreze, and R G Barry, *The Arctic Climate System* (Cambridge: Cambridge University Press, 2005).
[10] W S Broecker, 'The Great Ocean Conveyor', *Oceanography* (Vol. 4, 1991), pp. 79–89.
[11] O M Johannessen, E V Shalina and M W Miles, 'Satellite Evidence for an Arctic Sea Ice Cover in Transformation', *Science* (Vol. 286, 1999), pp. 1938–39.
[12] M G McPhee, A Proshutinsky, J H Morison, M Steele and M B Alkire, 'Rapid Change in Freshwater Content of the Arctic Ocean', L10602, *Geophysical Research Letters* (Vol. 36, 2009).
[13] J Comiso, 'A Rapidly Declining Perennial Sea Ice Cover in the Arctic', *Geophysical Research Letters* (Vol. 29, 2002), pp. 1956–60.

by several degrees.[14] Diminishing sea ice in the Arctic (Figure 3) is shrinking one of the Earth's major solar reflectors, which is a climate feedback that exacerbates the current warming.

The sea ice is also a primary habitat feature in the Arctic marine ecosystem. There are entire communities of microscopic plants and animals living on the underside of the sea ice in addition to the well-known 'charismatic megafauna' on the surface (such as the polar bear). Moreover, the sea ice influences the dynamics of populations in the underlying water as well as on the sea floor.

Figure 6: *See colour plate on p. 24.*

An indirect impact on the dynamics of the Arctic marine ecosystem, melting of the sea ice in the Arctic Ocean is decreasing the availability of calcium carbonate, which is necessary for species to precipitate shells.[15] The calcium carbonate is further impacted by ocean acidification due to increased concentrations of carbon dioxide absorbed into the seawater from the atmosphere.[16] The resulting under-saturation of calcium carbonate has implications for shell-building species in the water and on the sea floor that will impact associated and dependent biota.

More directly, under the sea ice, amphipods are consumed by arctic cod that, in turn, become the prey of belugas, narwhals, harp seals, ringed seals, bearded seals and hooded seals.[17] Changes in the sea-ice and amphipod populations will influence

---

[14] W D Sellers, 'A Global Climate Model Based on the Energy Balance of the Earth-atmosphere System', *Journal of Applied Meteorology* (Vol. 8, 1969), pp. 392–400.

[15] M Yamamoto-Kawai, F A McLaughlin, E C Carmack, S Nishino and K Shimada, 'Aragonite Undersaturation in the Arctic Ocean: Effects of Ocean Acidification and Sea Ice Melt', *Science* (Vol. 326, 2009), pp. 1098–1100.

[16] The Royal Society, *Ocean Acidification Due to Increasing Atmospheric Carbon Dioxide*, Policy Document 12/05 (London: The Royal Society, 2005).

[17] C T Tynan and D P DeMaster, 'Observations and Predictions of Arctic Climatic Change: Potential Effects on Marine Mammals', *Arctic* (Vol. 50, 1997), pp. 308–22.

Arctic cod populations with cascading consequences through the ecosystem.

In the Bering Sea, for example, decreasing sea-ice coverage is already influencing an ecosystem shift from Arctic to sub-Arctic conditions that favour species in the water column rather than on the sea floor.[18] Dependent populations of large bottom-feeding animals (such as spectacled eiders, grey whales and walruses) are relocating northward. Southern species are moving into the Bering Sea, causing additional faunal displacements that also will impact commercial and subsistence fisheries.

The poster child of decreasing Arctic sea-ice coverage is the polar bear, which, along with its bearded seal prey, is dependent on landfast coastal sea ice.[19] It is estimated that there are currently around 25,000 polar bears distributed over a maximum of 15 million km^2 of Arctic sea ice.[20] By the end of the twenty-first century, the refuge for sea-ice habitat may be in the Canadian archipelago and Greenland, 'affording these regions of the polar basin the greatest likelihood of sustaining viable polar bear populations'.[21] The polar bear as a symbol

---

[18] J M Grebmeier, J M Overland, S E Moore, E V Farley, E C Carmack, L W Cooper, K E Frey, J H Helle, F A McLaughlin and S L McNutt, 'A Major Ecosystem Shift in the Northern Bering Sea', *Science* (Vol. 311, 2006), pp. 1461–63.

[19] S C Amstrup, 'Polar bear: *Ursus maritimus*' in G A Feldhamer, B C Thompson and J A Chapman (eds), *Wild Mammals of North America: Biology, Management, and Conservation,* 2nd edition (Baltimore: Johns Hopkins University Press, 2003), pp. 587–610.

[20] J Aars, N J Lunn and A E Derocher (eds), 'Polar Bears: Proceedings of the 14th Working Meeting of the IUCN/SSC Polar Bear Specialist Group, 20–24 June 2005', Occasional Paper of the Species Survival Commission No. 32 (Washington: IUCN, 2006).

[21] G M Durner, D C Douglas, R M Nielson, S C Amstrup and T L McDonald, 'Predicting the Future Distribution of Polar Bear Habitat in the Polar Basin from Resource Selection Functions Applied to 21st Century General Circulation Model Projections of Sea Ice', USGS Science Strategy to Support US Fish and Wildlife Service Polar Bear Listing Decision (Reston, VI: US Geographical Survey, 2007), <http://www.usgs.gov/newsroom/special/polar_bears/docs/USGS_PolarBear_Durner_Habitat_lowres.pdf>.

(more so than even the indigenous populations) is awakening human concerns about the environmental state-change in the Arctic Ocean. Together – across a suite of physical, chemical, geological and biological processes – this fundamental shift from a permanent sea-ice cap to a seasonally ice-free sea has global implications in the Earth system across and beyond the boundaries of nations.

Global Society

The twentieth century is the point from when our civilisation truly emerged as a global society with transboundary perspectives and responsibilities (Figure 7). While the impact of human progress began extending around the world well beforehand (for example, in landscape transformations through agriculture) it was only with the animus of two World Wars that humankind was inexorably introduced to the interconnectedness among all nations and peoples on a planetary scale.

The hostilities of the Second World War were soon replaced on a global scale by the Cold War, with the nuclear superpowers of the United States and Soviet Union facing each other directly across the Arctic. By 1949, both nations possessed nuclear weapons that could be delivered by aeroplane. This clear and present danger stimulated the United States, starting in the early 1950s, to design and implement lines of Distance Early Warning (DEW) radar stations across the Arctic to detect incoming Russian bombers.[22]

The delicate tightrope between the United States and Soviet Union was stretched even further when nuclear submarines began criss-crossing under the Arctic sea-ice cap; the first was the USS *Nautilus*, which reached the North Pole in August 1958, providing the initial glimpse of under-ice topography.[23] Since the

---

[22] R F Naka and W W Ward, 'Distant Early Warning Line Radars: The Quest for Automatic Signal Detection', *Lincoln Laboratory Journal* (Vol. 12, 2000), pp. 181–204.

[23] A S McLaren, 'Analysis of the Under-Ice Topography in the Arctic Basin as Recorded by the USS *Nautilus* during August 1958', *Arctic* (Vol. 41, 1988), pp. 117–26.

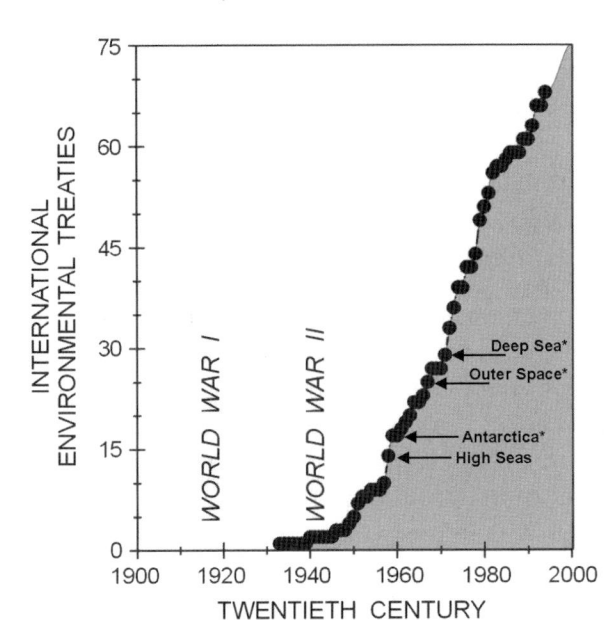

Figure 7: Emergence of Global Interdependence of our Civilisation during the Twentieth Century.[24]

Note: In stark contrast to the global conflicts of the two World Wars during the first half of the twentieth century, nearly 95 per cent of the multilateral ecosystem and environmental conventions and treaties in force were signed after 1950. Remote sensing and digital technologies, along with accelerated transport across the planet, also contributed to the transformation into a global society during the twentieth century. International legal frameworks to establish 'international spaces' beyond sovereign jurisdictions (arrows) originated with the High Seas in 1958. The 1959 Antarctic Treaty was the first nuclear arms agreement and the precedent for arms control regimes; * for outer space and the deep sea in 1967 and 1971, respectively (see Table 5 below).

early 1960s – with the addition of submarine-launched ballistic missiles (SLBMs) that could deliver nuclear weapons across continents – the persistent sea-ice cover across the Arctic Ocean has hidden precarious threats to global security.

---

[24] Modified from P A Berkman, *Science into Policy: Global Lessons from Antarctica* (London: Academic Press, 2002).

These military security issues of the Cold War were in contrast to the co-operation that had been developing in the region among Arctic and non-Arctic nations since 1920, following the adoption of the Treaty Concerning the Archipelago of Spitsbergen, and its Protocol:[25]

> DESIROUS, while recognising the sovereignty of Norway over the Archipelago of Spitsbergen, including Bear Island, of seeing these territories provided with an equitable regime, in order to assure their development and peaceful utilization.

Curiously, in the same manner that international spaces would emerge as a strategy for peace after the Second World War (Figure 7), the Treaty Concerning the Archipelago of Spitsbergen followed from the 'conditions or restrictions resulting from the war of 1914–1919'. **Today, there are forty-two parties to the 1920 Spitsbergen Treaty, involving all Arctic states as well as non-Arctic nations from every populated continent as a concrete demonstration of long-standing global participation in Arctic affairs (Table 3)**.

Around the world adoption of international agreements, such as the 1920 Spitsbergen Treaty, accelerated after the Second World War, with a transboundary focus on environmental and ecosystem issues (Figure 7) – as noted by the Nordic Council, which originated in 1952 'after the Second World War [when] the politicians of the time strived for stronger international co-operation'.[26] Moreover:[27]

> A large part of the Nordic land and sea areas lie in the Arctic region. The Nordic countries are therefore strongly involved in issues that concern this unique and harsh, but also vulnerable area.

---

[25] Treaty Concerning the Archipelago of Spitsbergen, and Protocol, 9 February 1920, <http://www.austlii.edu.au/au/other/dfat/treaties/1925/10.html>.

[26] Nordic Council, 'The History of the Nordic Council', <http://www.norden.org/en/nordic-council/the-nordic-council>, accessed 6 August 2010.

[27] Nordic Council, 'About the Nordic Co-operation in the Arctic', <http://www.norden.org/en/areas-of-co-operation/the-arctic>, accessed 6 August 2010.

Table 3 International Participation in Arctic Organisations[b]

	AC[c]	AMEC	AOSB	BEAC	FARO	IASC	NACGF	NC	NEAFC[4]	NF	OSPAR[4]	PB	SCPA	SPITS
Afghanistan														X
Albania														X
Argentina														X
Australia														X
Austria														X
Belgium[e]							X				X			X
Bulgaria[e]									X					X
Canada	X		X		X	X	X			X		X	X	X
Chile	X													X
China			X		X	X			X	X				X
Cuba														
Czech Republic[e]														X
Denmark[e,f]	X		X	X	X	X	X	X	X		X	X	X	X
Dominican Republic														X
Egypt														
Estonia[e]							X							X
Finland[e]	X		X	X	X	X	X	X	X	X	X	X	X	X
France[e]	X		X		X	X	X				X			X
Germany[e]	X		X		X	X	X				X			X
Greece[e]														X
Hungary[e]														X
Iceland	X		X	X	X	X	X	X	X	X	X		X	X
India														X
Ireland[e]							X				X			X
Italy[e]	X				X	X								X

Beyond National Boundaries

Table 3 (Continued)

	AC[c]	AMEC	AOSB	BEAC	FARO	IASC	NACGF	NC	NEAFC[4]	NF	OSPAR[4]	PB	SCPA	SPITS
Japan	X									X				
Korea (South)			X		X	X				X				X
Latvia[e]			X		X	X								
Lithuania							X							
Luxembourg[e]							X				X			
Monaco														X
Netherlands[e]	X				X	X					X			X
New Zealand							X							X
Norway	X	X	X	X	X	X	X	X	X	X	X	X	X	X
Poland[e]	X		X		X		X							X
Portugal[e]							X		X					X
Romania														
Russian Federation	X	X	X	X	X	X	X	X	X	X	X	X	X	X
Saudi Arabia														X
Serbia														X
South Africa														X
Spain[e]	X						X		X		X			X
Sweden[e]	X	X	X	X	X	X	X	X	X	X	X	X	X	X
Switzerland			X								X			X
United Kingdom[e]	X	X	X		X	X	X				X			X
United States	X	X	X	X	X	X	X	X	X	X	X	X	X	X
Venezuela														X

Table 3 (*Continued*)

	AC[c]	AMEC	AOSB	BEAC	FARO	IASC	NACGF	NC	NEAFC[d]	NF	OSPAR[d]	PB	SCPA	SPITS
Number of Nations	17	4	16	6	17	16	20	5	8	8	15	5	7	42

[a] Shaded nations are the eight Arctic states.

[b] **AC**: Arctic Council, 1996, <www.arctic-council.org/>; **AMEC**: Arctic Military Environmental Cooperation Programme, 1996, <www.mil.no/felles/ffi/amec>; **AOSB**: Arctic Ocean Sciences Board, 1984, <www.aosb.org/>; **BEAC**: Barents Euro-Arctic Council, 1993 <www.beac.st>; **FARO**: Forum of Arctic Research Operators, 1998, <www.faro-arctic.org/>; **IASC**: International Arctic Science Committee, 1990, <www.arcticportal.org/iasc/>; **NACGF**: North Atlantic Coast Guard Forum, 2007, <www.nacgf.com/>; **NC**: Nordic Council, 1952, <www.norden.org/en/nordic-council/>; **NEAFC**: Convention on Future Multilateral Cooperation in North-East Atlantic Fisheries, 1980, <http://www.neafc.org/>; **NF**: Northern Forum, 1991, <www.northernforum.org>; **OSPAR**: Convention for the Protection of the Marine Environment of the North-East Atlantic, 1992, <www.ospar.org>; **PB**: Agreement on the Conservation of Polar Bears, 1973, <http://pbsg.npolar.no/en/agreements/agreement1973.html>; **SCP**: Standing Committee of the Conference of Parliamentarians of the Arctic Region, 1994, <www.arcticparl.org/>; **SPITS**: Treaty Concerning the Archipelago of Spitsbergen, and Protocol 1920, <www.austlii.edu.au/au/other/dfat/treaties/1925/10.html>.

[c] Arctic Council includes the **member states** from the eight Arctic nations (shaded); permanent participants from the **indigenous peoples organisations** (Aluet International Association, <www.aleut-international.org>; Arctic Athabaskan Council, <www.arcticathabaskancouncil.com/>; Gwich'in Council International, <http://www.gwichin.org/>; Inuit Circumpolar Council, <http://www.inuit.org/>; Russian Association of Indigenous Peoples of the North, <www.raipon.org/>; and the Sámi Council, <www.saamicouncil.net/>; and both **permanent observers** and **ad hoc observers** that involve nation states as well as international organisations.

[d] Includes European Economic Community.

[e] Member of the European Union.

[f] Includes Greenland and the Faroe Islands as autonomous areas.

Similarly, because of their 'special responsibilities and special interests in the Arctic Region', the five coastal states adopted the 1973 Agreement on the Conservation of Polar Bears (Table 3).[28] This agreement to manage human impact on the polar bear population and to protect its ecosystem recognises 'that the polar bear is a significant resource of the Arctic Region which requires additional protection'.

The multi-national dimensions of environmental and ecosystem co-operation in the Arctic Ocean took another step with the 1959 North-East Atlantic Fisheries Convention, which was subsequently replaced by the 1980 Convention on Future Multilateral Cooperation in North-East Atlantic Fisheries (NEAFC).[29] With exceptions in the Baltic Sea and Mediterranean Sea:

> the Convention area shall be the waters within those parts of the Atlantic and Arctic Oceans and their dependent seas which lie north of 36° north latitude and between 42° west longitude and 51° east longitude ... and within that part of the Atlantic Ocean north of 59° north latitude and between 44° west longitude and 42° west longitude.

The objective of the NEAFC is to provide:[30]

> conservation and optimum utilization of such resources, and to recommend conservation measures in waters outside national jurisdiction.

Importantly, NEAFC encourages 'international co-operation and consultation with respect to these [fishery] resources'.

---

[28] Agreement on the Conservation of Polar Bears, Oslo, 15 November 1973, entry into force 26 May 1976, <http://pbsg.npolar.no/en/agreements/agreement1973.html>.

[29] Convention on Future Multilateral Cooperation in North-East Atlantic Fisheries, London, 18 November 1980, entry into force 17 March 1982, <http://www.neafc.org/>.

[30] FAO, Fisheries and Aquaculture Department, 'II.2.2 Northeast Atlantic Fisheries Commission: Main Objectives and Activities', <http://www.fao.org/docrep/w1310e/w1310e02.htm>, accessed 6 August 2010.

Starting with the 1972 Oslo Convention against marine dumping, and broadening with the 1974 Paris Convention that covered land-based sources as well as offshore industry, the agreements were unified into the 1992 Convention for the Protection of the Marine Environment of the North-East Atlantic (commonly known as OSPAR).[31] In 1998, OSPAR further adopted an annex on biodiversity and ecosystems to cover non-polluting human activities that can adversely affect the sea, recognising that:[32]

> concerted action at national, regional and global levels is essential to prevent and eliminate marine pollution and to achieve sustainable management of the maritime area, that is, the management of human activities in such a manner that the marine ecosystem will continue to sustain the legitimate uses of the sea and will continue to meet the needs of present and future generations.

The North-East Atlantic is defined by the NEAFC and OSPAR within exactly the same sector of latitudes and longitudes to the North Pole and with the same exclusions. However, more broadly than the 'waters' within the NEAFC, the inclusive and forward-looking scope of OSPAR applies broadly to the 'maritime area' involving:[33]

> the internal waters and the territorial seas of the Contracting Parties, the sea beyond and adjacent to the territorial sea under the jurisdiction of the coastal state to the extent recognised by international law, and the high seas, including the bed of all those waters and its sub-soil.

As with natural processes in the Earth system (see Figure 5), legal processes in international institutions (Table 3) connect the Arctic Ocean specifically with marine areas south of the Arctic Circle.

---

[31] Convention for the Protection of the Marine Environment of the North-East Atlantic, Paris, 22 September 1992, entry into force 25 March 1998, <http://www.ospar.org/html_documents/ospar/html/ OSPAR Convention_e_updated_text_2007.pdf>.
[32] Ibid.
[33] Ibid.

Beyond the international legal frameworks, a suite of international forums has also emerged to address environmental and ecosystem issues in the high north (Table 3). Many of these organisations are directly related to research activities, including the Ocean Sciences Board (1984), International Arctic Science Committee (1990), Northern Forum (1991) and Forum of Arctic Research Operators (1998). The Barents-Euro Arctic Council (1993), Standing Committee of the Conference of Parliamentarians of the Arctic Region (1994) and Arctic Council (1996) further provide diplomatic frameworks to assess the research implications. In addition, there is a targeted programme on Arctic Military Environmental Co-operation (1996) to 'address military-related environmental problems, primarily submarine dismantlement, in the fragile Arctic ecosystem of Russia's northwest'.[34]

The Arctic Council is a particularly important 'high level forum', which establishes that the eight Arctic states and indigenous peoples organisations have 'common Arctic issues, in particular issues of sustainable development and environmental protection.'[35] The only other Arctic-related institutions that involve all of the Arctic states are the 1920 Treaty Concerning the Archipelago of Spitsbergen, Standing Committee of the Conference of Parliamentarians of the Arctic Region and the North Atlantic Coast Guard Forum (Table 3).

While Table 3 is somewhat subjective in terms of the organisations included, it does offer a comparison of international collaboration by the Arctic states, ranked in terms of engagement: Norway, then Denmark, then Iceland and the Russian Federation, then Finland and Sweden, then the United States, and lastly Canada. The table further reveals engagement among forty-seven nations in Arctic affairs, especially regarding environmental and ecosystem issues, which have facilitated co-operation among nations and peoples on a global scale since the twentieth century (Figure 7).

---

[34] The Arctic Military Environmental Co-operation Group, <http://www.bellona.org/subjects/Amec>.

[35] Declaration on the Establishment of the Arctic Council, Ottowa, 19 September 1996, <http://www.international.gc.ca/polar-polaire/ottdec-decott.aspx?lang=en>.

International Spaces

After the Second World War, the international community established legal institutions to manage uninhabited regions beyond sovereign jurisdiction (Figure 7), creating the concept of 'international spaces' in the last half-century.[36] Today, 'international spaces' is a category of international law.[37] A landmark in the conceptualisation of international spaces was the United Nations Conference on the Law of the Sea that was convened by eighty-six nations from 24 February to 27 April 1958 in Geneva. It was designed to:[38]

> examine the law of the sea, taking account not only of the legal but also of the technical, biological, economic and political aspects of the problem and to embody the results of its work in one or more international conventions or such other instruments as it may deem appropriate.

This United Nations Conference resulted in four conventions regarding law of the sea (Table 4).[39] From these conventions, the first multilateral demarcation of an international space appeared, namely the 'High Seas'. As established by the 1958 Convention on the High Seas, they constitute 'all parts of the sea that are not included in the territorial sea or in the internal waters of a State'. Moreover:

> The high seas being open to all nations, no State may validly purport to subject any part of them to its Sovereignty. Freedom of the high seas is exercised under the conditions laid down by these articles and by the other rules of international law.

---

[36] J Kish, *The Law of International Spaces* (Leiden: A W Sijthoff International Publishing, 1971).
[37] International Law Commission of the United Nations, <http://untreaty.un.org/ilc/texts/texts.htm>.
[38] United Nations General Assembly Resolution 1105 (XI), 21 February 1957.
[39] T Treves, *Geneva Conventions on the Law of the Sea* (Geneva: United Nations Office of Legal Affairs, 1958), <http://untreaty.un.org/cod/diplomaticconferences/lawofthesea-1958/lawofthe-1958.html>.

As a legal construct, freedom of the seas had been evolving for centuries. Notably, the Dutch jurist, Hugo de Groot, wrote *Mare Liberum* in 1609 to describe certain freedoms beyond sovereign jurisdiction enjoyed by all humankind in the sea.[40] The Convention on the High Seas instantiated freedoms for navigating across, fishing in, laying submarine cables and pipelines under, and flying over the high seas. However, the Convention on the High Seas was adopted without any references to peace, security or stability in this international space.

During 1958, US President Dwight D Eisenhower invited eleven other countries, including the Soviet Union, to establish administrative arrangements 'dedicated to the principle that the vast uninhabited wastes of Antarctica shall be used only for peaceful purposes'.[41] On 1 December 1959 in Washington, DC, these twelve nations[42] signed the Antarctic Treaty – the first

Table 4: Law of the Sea Conventions Crafted in Geneva on 29 April 1958.

Convention Title	Entry into Force
Convention on the High Seas	30 September 1962
Convention on the Continental Shelf	10 June 1964
Convention on the Territorial Sea and the Contiguous Zone	10 September 1964
Convention on Fishing and Conservation of Living Resources	20 March 1966

Note: The four 1958 conventions have been superseded by the 1982 United Nations Convention on the Law of the Sea (UNCLOS), but they remain customary international law for those parties yet to ratify UNCLOS – most notably the United States.

---

[40] H Bull, B Kingsbury and A Roberts (eds), *Hugo Grotius and International Relations* (New York: Oxford University Press, 1990).

[41] D D Eisenhower, 'Statement by the President Concerning Antarctica', 3 May 1958.

[42] Original signatories to the Antarctic Treaty were seven claimant nations (Argentina, Australia, Chile, France, New Zealand, Norway, the United Kingdom) and five non-claimant nations (Belgium, Japan, South Africa, Union of Soviet Socialist Republics, the United States).

nuclear arms agreement – with application over the area south of 60°S, including all ice shelves:[43]

> Recognizing that it is in the interest of all mankind that Antarctica shall continue forever to be used exclusively for peaceful purposes and shall not become the scene or object of international discord.

Amidst the stockpiling of nuclear weapons[44] and Cold War posturing for a nuclear war,[45] President Eisenhower pursued peaceful alternatives to engage the Soviet Union. In 1955, he proposed 'Open Skies'[46] and when this strategy was unsuccessful, he promoted the 'Freedom of Space' for the launch of satellites during the International Geophysical Year (IGY),[47] which became the first United States space policy.[48]

President Eisenhower sought to establish the peaceful use of international spaces, starting with Antarctica (Table 5).[49] Well before the Antarctic Treaty had even been signed, President

---

[43] *Antarctic Treaty*, Washington, DC, 1 December 1959, entry into force 23 June 1961, <http://www.atsummit50.aq>.

[44] D A Rosenberg, 'The Origins of Overkill: Nuclear Weapons and American Strategy, 1945–1960', *International Security* (Vol. 7, No. 4, 1983), pp. 3–71.

[45] H A Kissinger, *Nuclear Weapons and Foreign Policy* (New York: Harper & Brothers, 1957).

[46] D D Eisenhower, '"Open Skies" Proposal', 21 July 1955, Public Papers of the Presidents: Dwight D Eisenhower, *Documents of American History II*, pp. 713–16.

[47] The third International Polar Year was renamed the International Geophysical Year and convened by the International Council of Scientific Unions from 1 July 1957 through 31 December 1958.

[48] National Security Council, 'U.S. Scientific Satellite Program', NSC 5520 (Washington, DC: National Security Council, 1955).

[49] P A Berkman, 'President Eisenhower, the Antarctic Treaty and Origin of International Spaces' in Paul A Berkman, M A Lang, D W H Walton and O R Young (eds), *Science Diplomacy: Antarctica, Science and the Governance of International Spaces* (Washington, DC: Smithsonian Institution Scholarly Press, forthcoming 2010).

Table 5: Initial Agreements to Establish International Spaces beyond Sovereign Jurisdictions in the High Seas, Antarctica, Outer Space and the Deep Sea.

Agreement Name	Location and Date of Signature	Entry into Force	Peaceful Purposes	Arms Control Provisions
Convention on the High Seas	Geneva 29 April 1958	30 September 1962	Not Specified	No
Antarctic Treaty	Washington, DC 1 December 1959	23 June 1961	'Matters of common interest'	Yes
Treaty on Principles Governing the Activities of States in the Exploration and Use of Outer Space, Including the Moon and other Celestial Bodies (Outer Space Treaty)	London, Moscow Washington, DC 27 January 1967	10 October 1967	'Common interest of all mankind'	Yes
Treaty on the Prohibition of the Emplacement of Nuclear Weapons and Other Weapons of Mass Destruction on the Seabed and the Ocean Floor and in the Subsoil (Deep-Sea Treaty)	London, Moscow Washington, DC 11 February 1971	18 May 1972	'Common interest of mankind'	Yes

Eisenhower recognised that international governance of Antarctica was directly relevant to outer space:[50]

> If, by analogy to the Antarctic proposal of the United States, international agreement can be reached in space and the rules and regulations to be followed with respect thereto, problems of sovereignty may be avoided or at least deferred.

The IGY itself demonstrated the role of science as a tool of diplomacy in facilitating co-operation between the United States and Soviet Union at the height of the Cold War. Among its many achievements, it is perhaps most remarkable that the IGY enabled these two Cold War adversaries to peacefully launch 'a small scientific satellite under international auspices', even though this 'demonstration of advanced technology' had an 'unmistakable relationship with intercontinental ballistic missile technology'.[51]

The freedom of space was subsequently instituted in the 1967 Outer Space Treaty that was signed in London, Moscow and Washington, DC (Table 5). Moreover, following the Antarctic Treaty, the Outer Space Treaty became the second agreement with nuclear arms control provisions followed by the 1971 Seabed Treaty that was also signed in London, Moscow and Washington, DC (Table 5). The three nuclear powers of the time (the UK, USSR and USA) were explicitly expressing the 'common interests of mankind' to use the international spaces of the seabed, outer space and Antarctica exclusively for 'peaceful purposes'. The high seas, however, remain without the non-armament and peaceful-use provisions of the other international spaces.

After the Second World War, nations recognised that diverse transboundary processes and phenomena influenced their own security. This international awareness has been reflected by the growth of environmental and ecosystem regimes (Figure 7), as well as the emergence of international spaces for global co-operation beyond national interests alone

---

[50] National Security Council, 'U.S. Policy on Outer Space', NSC 5814 (Washington, DC: National Security Council, 1958).
[51] National Security Council, 'U.S. Scientific Satellite Program', NSC 5520 (Washington, DC: National Security Council, 1955).

(Table 5).[52] Even so, with increasing technological development and estimates of potential resources, nations will pursue their national interests in these international spaces:[53]

> The high seas, the deep ocean and the polar regions are likely to become areas of increased competition as advanced technology, increased accessibility and resource pressure encourage more intensive exploitation by states and commercial interests. Competition will centre on fishing, deep sea mining and the extraction of oil and gas, but may possibly extend to transportation and rights of passage.

We live in a unique period when benefits for humankind will be increasingly derived from the use of international spaces (Table 5), which cover nearly 70 per cent of the Earth's surface, as opposed to the territories of nation-states that cover the remaining area. Consequently, we are living during a profound transition of governance during a time when the decisions made today on international spaces will have global implications well into the future. Most notably, in response to climate change, states and international organisations are now considering management strategies that require unprecedented co-ordination among human populations on a planetary scale.[54]

Moreover, we are living during a special period with unparalleled capacity to assess impacts across the Earth on a real-time basis, with increasing clarity of historical contexts and future circumstances. The environmental state-change, however, is introducing a new Arctic Ocean system that will require enhanced international capacity and co-ordination to assess the potential instabilities, as illustrated with reference to the Arctic marine ecosystem (Figure 6):[55]

---

[52] P A Berkman, 'International Spaces Promote Peace', *Nature* (Vol. 462, 2009), pp. 412–13.
[53] Joint Doctrine and Concepts Board, *The Future Maritime Operational Concept* (Shrivenham: Development, Concepts and Doctrine Centre, 2007), pp. 1–4.
[54] *United Nations Framework Convention on Climate Change*, <http://unfccc.int/>.
[55] J M Grebmeier, S E Moore, J E Overland, K E Frey and R Gradinger, 'Biological Responses to Recent Pacific Arctic Sea Ice Retreats', *Transactions of the American Geophysical Union* (Vol. 91, No. 18, 2010), p. 161.

The Arctic is no longer predictable. Clear changes in the ecosystem from plankton to polar bears are evident. It is critical that biological measurements be included in international ocean-observing systems to track and forecast the fate of Arctic marine ecosystems.

International spaces introduce legal frameworks and infrastructures based largely on common interests that can be used to balance the national interests, which have otherwise motivated and divided states throughout history. **With its national and international spaces, the Arctic Ocean is a case study for humankind that will set precedents for balancing national interests and common interests elsewhere.**

4. MATTERS OF SECURITY

Political Stability

At the heart of security matters are risks to political, economic and cultural stability. These risks are intertwined and underlie urgent decisions that individuals, institutions and governments make about allocating finite resources and assets.

Like any environmental state-change, the transformation of the sea-ice boundary condition of the Arctic Ocean (Figure 3) introduces risks of instabilities. As noted by Javier Solana (then High Representative for the Common Foreign and Security Policy, Secretary-General of the Council of the European Union) in March 2008: 'Climate change is best viewed as a threat multiplier which exacerbates existing trends, tensions and instability'.[1]

Some of the instabilities will be predictable and may even have positive features, such as opportunities to produce new energy, fishing or shipping industries. Other instabilities will be unanticipated and non-linear with negative consequences. The challenge in all cases is to thoughtfully consider the risks of instabilities with as much foresight as possible so that appropriate responses can be identified and then implemented.

The Gorbachev Principles

Risks in the Arctic have been addressed previously, well before humankind was introduced to the environmental state-change in the Arctic Ocean. In 1987, at the end of the Cold War, President of

---

[1] J Solana, 'Climate Change and International Security', Paper from the High Representative and the European Commission to the European Council, S113/08, 14 March 2008, <http://www.consilium.europa.eu/uedocs/cms_data/docs/pressdata/en/reports/99387.pdf>.

the Soviet Union, Mikhail Gorbachev, invited 'the countries of the region to a discussion on the burning security issues', noting:[2]

> The community and interrelationship of the interests of our entire world is felt in the northern part of the globe, in the Arctic, perhaps more than anywhere else. For the Arctic and the North Atlantic are not just the 'weather kitchen', the point where cyclones and anticyclones are born to influence the climate in Europe, the USA and Canada, and even in South Asia and Africa.

This seminal speech, coming as it did at the end of the Cold War, resonated among nations, encouraging the mitigation of political instabilities in the Arctic. President Gorbachev also offered some solutions to promote co-operation and prevent conflict in the Arctic with the following six recommendations, which provide baselines to evaluate progress in addressing political, economic and cultural instabilities in the Arctic Ocean today:[3]

1. 'A nuclear-free zone in Northern Europe
2. Restricting naval activity in the seas ... of Northern Europe
3. Peaceful cooperation in developing the resources of the North, the Arctic
4. Scientific exploration of the Arctic is of immense importance for the whole of mankind ... setting up a joint Arctic Research Council
5. Cooperation of the northern countries in environmental protection; and
6. Open the Northern Sea Route to foreign ships, with ourselves providing the services of ice-breakers.'

While developing a 'nuclear-free zone in Northern Europe' was not feasible, there was substantive progress at the time

---

[2] Mikhail Gorbachev, 'Speech in Murmansk at the Ceremonial Meeting on the Occasion of the Presentation of the Order of Lenin and the Gold Star to the City of Murmansk, 1 October 1987', English translation prepared by the Press Office of the USSR Embassy, Ottawa, 1988, <http://www.barentsinfo.fi/docs/Gorbachev_speech.pdf>.

[3] *Ibid.*

through the Treaty on the Reduction and Limitation of Strategic Offensive Arms (START I).[4] Following negotiations going back to 1982, START 1 was signed in Moscow on 31 July 1991 by President George H W Bush and President Gorbachev, just before the 25 December 1991 dissolution of the Soviet Union and the end of the Cold War.[5]

In addition to the 'nuclear-free zone', the Gorbachev speech also suggested that the 'North of the globe, the Arctic, become a zone of peace'. This juxtaposition of 'zones' confuses the issue because peace has been equated with demilitarisation – in other words, the long-standing 'tendency of American political leaders to define security problems and their solutions in military terms'.[6] Moreover, demilitarisation in the Arctic Ocean would not be feasible with Russia's Northern Fleet being based there. Nonetheless, underlying the rationale for strategic deployments, peace is the fundamental common interest.

Similarly, 'restricting naval activities' has not been feasible. The United States, for example, has long considered it vital to protect 'essential security interests in the Arctic, including preservation of the principle of freedom of the seas and superjacent airspace'.[7] This National Security Council statement in 1971 followed the 1969 voyage of the 115,000-ton USS *Manhattan* through the Northwest Passage (as shown in archived video[8]). Since that time, Canada has been asserting that the Canadian archipelago is 'internal waters' where they can

---

[4] Federation of American Scientists, 'Strategic Arms Reduction Treaty (START I) Chronology', <http://www.fas.org/nuke/control/start1/chron.htm>, accessed 5 August 2010.

[5] J L Gaddis, 'International Relations Theory and the End of the Cold War', *International Security* (Vol. 17, No. 3, 1992), pp. 5–58.

[6] R H Ullman, 'Redefining Security', *International Security* (Vol. 8, No. 1, 1983), pp. 129–53.

[7] National Security Council, 'National Security Decision Memorandum 144', United States Arctic Policy and Arctic Policy Group, 22 December 1971, <http://www.fas.org/irp/offdocs/nsdm-nixon/nsdm-144.pdf>.

[8] N Depoe, 'Breaking the Ice: Canada and the Northwest Passage', 8 September 1969, CBC Digital Archives, <http://archives.cbc.ca/science_technology/transportation/topics/2349-13648/>.

prevent passage,[9] whereas the United States has been contending that the region is an international strait open to 'transit passage' which shall not be impeded under law of the sea.[10]

This ongoing disagreement with regard to transit through the Northwest Passage also involves interpretations of 'innocent passage' that 'is not prejudicial to the peace, good order or security of the coastal State'.[11] On the opposite side of the Arctic Ocean, the concept of opening the 'North Sea Route to foreign ships' with ice-breaker services from Russia was somewhat clairvoyant, given the subsequent reduction in ice extent that enabled the September 2009 transit from South Korea to the Netherlands across the Northeast Passage along the northern coast of Russia by the Beluga vessels *Fraternity* and *Foresight*.[12]

Development of Co-operation Mechanisms
There was also strong support of Gorbachev's recommendation of 'scientific exploration', which triggered the establishment of the International Arctic Science Committee (IASC) in 1990 to produce 'leading-edge multi-disciplinary research to foster a greater scientific understanding of the arctic region and its role in the Earth system'.[13]

Today, the IASC is an international associate of the International Council for Science[14] with membership from all eight of the Arctic states plus an additional eleven nations (see Table 3). Importantly, 'cooperation of the northern countries in

---

[9] A Charon, 'The Northwest Passage in Context', *Canadian Military Journal* (Winter 2005–2006), pp. 41–48.
[10] J Kraska, 'The Law of the Sea Convention and the Northwest Passage', *International Journal for Marine and Coastal Law* (Vol. 22, 2007), pp. 257–81.
[11] EvREsearch Ltd, 'Law of the Sea Searchable Database', <http://lawofthesea.tierit.com>.
[12] A Smith, 'Global Warming Reopens the Northeast Passage', *TIME*, 17 September 2009.
[13] International Arctic Science Committee, <http://www.arcticportal.org/iasc/>.
[14] International Council for Science, <http://www.icsu.org>.

environmental protection' began to take form, complementing strategies that had been evolving around the world since the Second World War (Figure 6). On 12 January 1989, Finland invited the Arctic countries to formalise a solution for the Arctic,[15] which resulted in the Arctic Environmental Protection Strategy that was adopted by the eight Arctic states with the Rovaniemi Declaration on 14 June 1991:[16]

> Management, planning and development activities shall provide for the conservation, sustainable utilization and protection of Arctic ecosystems and natural resources for the benefit and enjoyment of present and future generations, including indigenous peoples.

In addition, there was synergy with the United Nations World Commission on Environment and Development, which had conceptualised a path between environmental protection and economic development under the rubric of sustainable development. The report issued in 1987 under the chairmanship of Norwegian Prime Minister Gro Harlem Brundtland[17] provides a framework to address 'the accelerating deterioration of the human environment and natural resources and the consequences of that deterioration for economic and social development'.[18]

Seeking to establish sustainable development in the Arctic – balancing environmental protection, economic prosperity and social equity – the Northern Forum (Table 3) was initiated in 1991, declaring at its first General Assembly in 1993:[19]

---

[15] O R Young, *Creating Regimes: Arctic Accords and International Governance* (New York: Cornell University Press, 1998).

[16] *Declaration on the Protection of Arctic Environment: Arctic Environmental Protection Strategy*, Rovaniemi, Finland, 14 June 1991, <http://arctic-council.org/filearchive/artic_environment.pdf>.

[17] United Nations World Commission on Environment and Development, *Our Common Future* (Oxford: Oxford University Press, 1987).

[18] United Nations General Assembly, *Report of the World Commission on Environment and Development*, Resolution 42/187, 11 December 1987, <http://www.un-documents.net/a42r187.htm>.

[19] *Declaration of the First General Assembly of the Northern Forum*, Tromsø, 3 October 1993, <http://www.northernforum.org/servlet/download?id=452>.

> [The] people of the North, through joint knowledge and efforts, are essential partners on the local, national and international level in both the protection of the Northern environment and the sustainable development, as defined in the Bruntland Commission Report, of our regions.

Also in 1993 – 'to provide impetus to existing cooperation and consider new initiatives and proposals' in the Barents Sea region[20] – the Barents Euro-Arctic Council was established (see Table 3). Moreover, the first Conference of Parliamentarians of the Arctic Region (Table 3) was convened in Reykjavik, Iceland that year.[21] All of these co-operation initiatives were taking root because of circumpolar partnerships that had become possible following the key inclusion of Russia after dissolution of the Soviet Union.

In a strategic manner, environmental protection also involved military assets, as demonstrated by the Arctic Military Environmental Cooperation programme (Table 3) that began with the United States, Russian Federation and Norway in 1996 and was extended to include the United Kingdom in 2003, 'underscoring the vital importance of cooperation between military organizations to prevent and solve environmental problems in the Arctic caused by their activities'.[22]

The Arctic Council
Progress with environmental protection and sustainable development opened the doors for an 'Arctic Research Council', borrowing from the success of the Scientific Committee on

---

[20] Barents Euro-Arctic Council, <http://www.beac.st/>.
[21] Conference of Parliamentarians of the Arctic Region, <http://www.arcticparl.org/>.
[22] Declaration among the Department of Defense of the United States of America, the Royal Ministry of Defence of the Kingdom of Norway, and the Ministry of Defence of the Russian Federation, on Arctic Military Environmental Cooperation, Bergen, Norway, 26 September 1996.

Antarctic Research that had facilitated international co-operation continuously in the south-polar region since the height of the Cold War in the late 1950s.[23]

The notion of a joint Arctic Research Council laid the foundation for the Declaration on the Establishment of the Arctic Council that was adopted in Ottawa, Canada, on 19 September 1996.[24] The 1996 Ottawa Declaration was approved by all eight Arctic states as members (see Table 3) along with six indigenous peoples organisations as permanent participants (Aleut International Association, Arctic Athabaskan Council, Gwich'in Council International, Inuit Circumpolar Council, Russian Association of Indigenous Peoples of the North, and Sámi Council) as a 'high level forum to':[25]

> provide a means for promoting cooperation, coordination and interaction among the Arctic States, with the involvement of the Arctic indigenous communities and other Arctic inhabitants on common arctic issues,* in particular issues of sustainable development and environmental protection in the Arctic.

The asterisk denotes that the 'Arctic Council should not deal with matters related to military security'.[26]

Emanating from the 1991 Rovaneimi Declaration[27] that established the Arctic Environmental Protection Strategy, the principal features of the Arctic Council are its working groups:[28]

- Arctic Monitoring and Assessment Program (AMAP)
- Protection of the Arctic Marine Environment (PAME)

---

[23] V Golitsyn, personal communication, 2009; E C H Keskitalo, *Negotiating the Arctic: The Construction of an International Region* (New York: Routledge, 2004).

[24] Declaration on the Establishment of the Arctic Council, Ottawa, 19 September 1996, <http://www.international.gc.ca/polar-polaire/ottdec-decott.aspx>.

[25] *Ibid.*

[26] *Ibid.*

[27] Declaration on the Protection of Arctic Environment, *op. cit.*

[28] Arctic Council Working Groups, <http://arctic-council.org/section/working_groups>.

- Arctic Contaminants Action Program (ACAP)
- Conservation of Arctic Fauna and Flora (CAFF)
- Emergency Prevention, Preparedness and Response (EPPR)
- Sustainable Development Working Group (SDWG).

Principal products of the Arctic Council's working groups include the:

- 1997 State of the Arctic Environment Report[29]
- 2002 Radioactivity in the Arctic Report[30]
- 2004 Arctic Climate Impact Assessment[31]
- 2004 Arctic Human Development Report[32]
- 2008 Arctic Oil and Gas Assessment[33]
- 2009 Human Health in the Arctic Report[34]
- 2009 Arctic Marine Shipping Assessment.[35]

As a high-level forum 'without legal personality',[36] or regulatory authority to develop binding policies, the Arctic Council has achieved considerable success in generating policy-relevant knowledge about the Arctic and bringing Arctic issues to the attention of global forums that include the: 2001 Stockholm Convention on Persistent Organic Pollutants, 2002 World Summit on Sustainable Development, and the 15th

---

[29] AMAP, 'Arctic Pollution Issues: A State of the Arctic Environment Report' (Oslo: AMAP, 1997).
[30] AMAP, 'AMAP Assessment 2002: Radioactivity in the Arctic' (Oslo: AMAP, 2004).
[31] AMAP, *Arctic Climate Impact Assessment* (Cambridge: Cambridge University Press, 2004).
[32] *Arctic Human Development Report* (Akureyri: Stefansson Arctic Institute, 2004), <http://www.svs.is/AHDR/AHDR%20chapters/English%20version/Chapters%20PDF.htm>.
[33] AMAP, 'Arctic Oil and Gas Assessment 2007' (Oslo: AMAP, 2008).
[34] AMAP, 'Human Health in the Arctic' (Oslo: AMAP, 2009).
[35] PAME, 'Arctic Marine Shipping Assessment Report 2009' (Trømso: Arctic Council, 2009).
[36] E T Bloom, 'Establishment of the Arctic Council', *American Journal of International Law* (Vol. 93, 1999), pp. 712–22.

Conference of the Parties (CoP15) to the United Nations Framework Convention on Climate Change in 2009.[37]

Peace in the Arctic
While the 1996 Ottawa Declaration promotes co-operation and identifies 'common arctic issues' among all Arctic states and indigenous peoples, 'peace' as an explicit common interest is absent. This omission was intentional, recognising that the concept of 'peace' had been on the table since 1991:[38]

> The peace and security of the Arctic must be advanced through means other than the militarization of the region. Significant here is the capacity of non-military cooperation among the arctic countries to create a climate of trust and confidence and the custom of co-operation, whereby military matters may be addressed directly and effectively.

Moreover, the purpose of the Arctic Council was first suggested in 1992:[39]

> To facilitate cooperation generally among its members, and in particular, with respect to the following matters: protection of the environment, coordination of scientific research, conservation of living resources, economic development, health and well-being of the Arctic inhabitants, and peaceful uses of the Arctic.

All of these principles were ultimately adopted in the 1966 Ottawa Declaration, except the 'peaceful' uses of the Arctic, as identified in the Ottawa Declaration preamble:[40]

---

[37] 'Tromsø Declaration on the Occasion of the Sixth Ministerial Meeting of The Arctic Council', Tromsø, Norway, 29 April 2009, <http://arctic-council.org/filearchive/Tromsoe%20Declaration-1..pdf>.
[38] Arctic Council Panel, 'To Establish an International Arctic Council: A Framework Report, 1991', <http://www.carc.org/pubs/v19no2/2.htm>.
[39] D Pharand, 'The Case for an Arctic Region Council and a Treaty Proposal', *Revue Générale de Droit* (Vol. 23, 1992), pp. 163–95.
[40] Declaration on the Establishment of the Arctic Council, Ottawa, Canada, 1996, <http://www.international.gc.ca/polar-polaire/ottdec-decott.aspx?lang=en>.

- 'well-being of the inhabitants of the Arctic'
- 'special relationship to the arctic of indigenous people and their communities'
- 'sustainable development in the Arctic region'
- 'protection of the Arctic environment'
- 'research to the collective understanding of the circumpolar Arctic.'

Without active shared dialogues to prevent conflict, it is a matter of serendipity that tensions in the Arctic region have been low since the Cold War. Nonetheless, there is a low threshold to establish shared dialogue that will both promote co-operation and prevent conflict in the Arctic Ocean.

The elephant in the room – the risk that has been avoided – is the long-standing presence of strategic military assets in the Arctic Ocean. To illustrate this fact, consider the 15 July 2009 report in the Russian newspaper, *Ria Novosti*:[41]

> Russia carried out test launches of two Sineva intercontinental ballistic missiles from two Delta IV class nuclear-powered submarines in service with the Northern Fleet, located under ice floe near the North Pole.

There was scant mention of these launches in the Western media. *Jane's Defence Weekly* indicated that these test launches were 'routine', which was the reason they did not report them, but that the Russian source was credible.[42] Submarine-Launched Ballistic Missile (SLBM) testing has been ongoing in the Arctic Ocean since 1961 and the number of reported test launches markedly increased after 1990 with the most recent Sineva SLBM launch in the Barents Sea on 4 March 2010 (Figure 8).

Routine or not, there appears to be a serious case of misplaced media priorities when Russian SLBM tests near the North Pole are treated as business-as-usual whereas a private expedition placing a Russian flag on the sea floor at the North Pole[43]

---

[41] *Ria Novosti*, 'Russian Outwitted U.S. Strategic Defenses with Missile Test', 15 July 2009.

[42] Personal communication with D Richardson of *Jane's Defence Weekly*, 20–21 July 2009.

[43] *BBC News*, 'Russia Plants Flag Under North Pole', 2 August 2007.

Environmental Security in the Arctic Ocean

ignites a global media frenzy – a century after the United States planted its flag on the ice-cap at the North Pole.[44] The lack of reporting may be because SLBMs launched from the Arctic Ocean could reach targets across Europe, Asia and North America unimpeded – reflecting the ongoing risk of mutually assured destruction.[45]

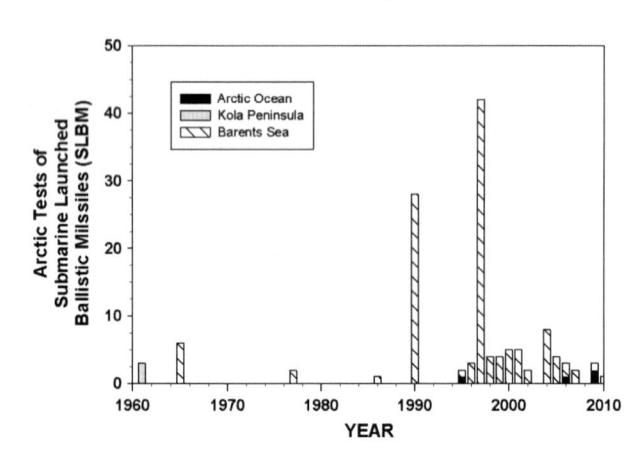

Figure 8: SLBM tests in the Arctic Ocean, 1960–2010.

Note: Unclassified data in 2007 includes associated information about the missile types, apogees, sites and missions.[46] The 2009 and 2010 SLBM launches were announced in *Ria Novosti*.[47] This figure shows 128 SLBM tests that have been publicly reported in the Arctic Ocean and may underestimate the actual number of tests.

---

[43] *BBC News*, 'Russia Plants Flag Under N Pole', 2 August 2007.
[44] *National Geographic News Watch*, 'Peary and the North Pole 100 years ago today', 6 April 2009, <http://blogs.nationalgeographic.com/blogs/news/chiefeditor/2009/04/peary-and-the-north-pole.html>.
[45] K A Lieber and D G Press, 'The Rise of U.S. Nuclear Primacy', *Foreign Affairs* (March/April 2006).
[46] Encyclopedia Aeronautica, 'Arctic Ocean Chronology', <http://www.astronautix.com/sites/arcocean.htm>.
[47] *Ria Novosti*, 'Russia Test Launches Second Sineva Ballistic Missile in two days', 18 July 2009.

At the end of the Cold War, military issues in the Arctic Ocean were well known and discussed prominently.[48] In view of the 'burning security issues' that remain – there is no room for complacency – such risks and instabilities 'that have accumulated in the area should be resolved above all'.[49] However, it is not about Russia or the United States or any other country that may have strategic interests in the Arctic Ocean. The fact is that SLBM or other such military assets for national security purposes in the Arctic Ocean are no less dangerous today than they were during the Cold War. In effect, the Cold War never ended in the Arctic Ocean.[50]

Matters of Common Interest: Polar Comparisons
There are two sides of the coin of peace – promote co-operation and prevent conflict – and neither is sufficient without the other. This lesson is perhaps best illustrated by the 1959 Antarctic Treaty, which recognises 'that it is in the interest of all mankind that Antarctica shall continue forever to be used exclusively for peaceful purposes and shall not become the scene or object of international discord'.[51]

The Antarctic Treaty identified 'matters of common interest' with science as the keystone.[52] As a parallel, the Arctic Council identified 'common Arctic issues'. Similarly, the Scientific Committee on Antarctic Research provided a template for the Arctic Council. Unfortunately, these science diplomacy precedents and lessons of international co-operation from Antarctica[53] have

---

[48] K Atland, 'Mikhail Gorbachev, the Murmansk Initiative, and the Desecuritization of Interstate Relations in the Arctic', *Cooperation and Conflict* (Vol. 43, No. 3, 2008), pp. 289–311.

[49] Gorbachev, *op. cit.*

[50] M Wallace and S Staples, 'Ridding the Arctic of Nuclear Weapons: A Task Long Overdue', Canadian Pugwash Group, 2010, <http://www.arcticsecurity.org/docs/arctic-nuclear-report-web.pdf>.

[51] The Antarctic Treaty, signed 1 December 1959, entry into force 23 June 1961.

[52] P A Berkman, *Science into Policy: Global Lessons from Antarctica* (London: Academic Press, 2002).

[53] Antarctic Treaty Summit, 'Science-Policy Interactions in International Governance in 2009 reflecting on lessons learned from the first fifty years of the 1959 Antarctic Treaty', <http://www.atsummit50.aq>.

been downplayed consistently by the Arctic states,[54] who still view the Arctic Ocean through a Cold War lens:[55]

> Due to its strategic importance, the Arctic, unlike Antarctica, has been a venue for Cold War competition. These are some of the reasons why an Antarctic-like Treaty that provided for complete demilitarization, freezing of territorial claims, and freedom of scientific research will not likely be concluded for the Arctic.

Indeed, there are substantive differences between the two polar regions, obviating the consideration of any treaty for the Arctic (see Table 6). As the Arctic coastal states indicated in their 2008 Ilulissat Declaration, they 'see no need to develop a new comprehensive international legal regime to govern the Arctic Ocean'.[56] However, such conclusions on governance dismiss the lessons of the Antarctic, which could help to promote co-operation and prevent conflict in the Arctic Ocean. On the other hand, it is practical as well as politically expedient to avoid discussions about comprehensive governance until after there is a common understanding of the risks and appropriate responses to the potential instabilities in the Arctic Ocean region.

While there are active and successful strategies for co-operation (Table 3), an inclusive focus to prevent conflict in the Arctic Ocean is absent. The risk of even mentioning military assets is that Arctic states will consider the dialogue in terms of military security issues. The reality is, however, that security issues in the Arctic Ocean are much broader than military security and that holistic strategies to address the potential instabilities are required.

Poignantly, as in the 1996 Ottawa Declaration, peace is absent in the 2008 Ilulissat Declaration that the five Arctic coastal states used to declare their 'stewardship role'. **How can lasting**

---

[54] D R Rothwell, *The Polar Regions and the Development of International Law* (Cambridge: Cambridge University Press, 1996).

[55] K S Yalowitz, J F Collins and R A Virginia, *The Arctic Climate Change and Security Policy Conference: Final Report and Findings* (Washington, DC: Carnegie Endowment for International Peace, 2009).

[56] The Ilulissat Declaration from the Arctic Ocean Conference, Ilulissat, Greenland, 28 May 2008, <http://www.oceanlaw.org/downloads/arctic/Ilulissat_Declaration.pdf>.

Table 6: Comparison of Arctic and Antarctic Characteristics.

Characteristic	Arctic	Antarctic
Location	The high-latitude region surrounding the North Pole (90°N)	The low-latitude region surrounding the South Pole (90°S)
Geography	Ocean surrounded by continents	Continent surrounded by ocean
Ecosystems	Strongly influenced by solar cycle poleward of Arctic Circle (66.5°N)	Strongly influenced by solar cycle poleward of Antarctic Circle (66.5°S)
Sea Ice	Year-round, mostly multi-year	Seasonal, mostly annual
Continental Shelf	Broadest, shallowest on Earth	Narrowest, deepest on Earth[a]
Humans	Indigenous people over millennia	No indigenous people
Science	International Arctic Science Committee	Scientific Committee on Antarctic Research
Territories	Recognised sovereignties	Claims to sovereignty[a]
Access	Restricted	Unrestricted
Living Resources	Ongoing exploitation	Ongoing exploitation
Mineral Resources	Ongoing exploitation	Exploitation prohibited
Ecotourism	Extensive	Extensive
Military Presence	Extensive since the Second World War	Non-militarised region
Nuclear Weapons	Extensive since the Second World War	Nuclear-Free Zone
Common Interests	Sustainable development and environmental protection[b]	(a) peaceful purposes only; (b) facilitation of scientific research; (c) facilitation of international scientific co-operation; (d) facilitation of the exercise of the rights of inspection; (e) questions relating to the exercise of jurisdiction; (f) preservation and conservation of living resources[c]
Legal Framework	Law of the Sea (Table 2)[d]	1959 Antarctic Treaty (Table 5)[e]

[a] Described and mapped in Berkman, *op. cit.*

[b] Defined as 'common arctic issues' in the 1996 Declaration on the Establishment of the Arctic Council, <http://www.international.gc.ca/polar-polaire/ottdec-decott.aspx?lang=en>.

[c] Defined as 'matters of common interest' in the 1959 Antarctic Treaty, Article IX.1, <http://www.ats.aq/documents/ats/treaty_original.pdf>.

[d] As expressed in the 2008 Ilulissat Declaration, the five Arctic coastal states 'remain committed' to the law of the sea, <http://www.oceanlaw.org/downloads/arctic/Ilulissat_Declaration.pdf>. The Arctic states have all adopted the 1982 UNCLOS Searchable Database, <http://lawofthesea.tierit.com>, with the exception of the United States.

[e] Antarctic Treaty Searchable Database, <http://aspire.tierit.com>.

peace and stability be achieved in the Arctic among all nations and peoples if these concepts are actively avoided in high-level forums? The answer to this question underlies the justification for an environmental security approach to address the diverse risks of instability associated with the environmental state-change in the Arctic Ocean, complementing the 'common Arctic issues' of sustainable development and environmental protection.

Economic Stability

Transboundary processes that cross sovereign jurisdictions are widely characterised in terms of security: climate security, economic security, energy security, environmental security, food security, human security, information security and the like. In addition, there are international spaces that exist beyond sovereign jurisdictions (see Table 5). In this arena of interests that transcend national boundaries, the environmental state-change in the Arctic Ocean (Figure 3) will open economic opportunities as a 'Resource Frontier Region'[57] with global ramifications.

As a region, Arctic economic production currently exceeds $230 billion per year (Table 7). These economic activities are based primarily on large-scale resource exploitation of fish, metallic minerals and fossil fuels.

Another characteristic of the Arctic economy is that family-based fishing, hunting, breeding and gathering activities continue to be important. Manufacturing in the Arctic is limited, but there is a strong service sector that involves retail, transport and tourism as well as education, healthcare and public administration. There are also marked changes in the service sector as indicated by the size of the tourism industry, which has grown from around 1 million tourists per year in the early 1990s to more than 1.5 million per

---

[57] D Sugden, *Arctic and Antarctic: A Modern Geographical Synthesis* (Oxford: Blackwell, 1982).

Table 7: Economic Production by the Arctic States in the Arctic Region.[a,b]

	Total Arctic Production ($ million)[c]	Percentage of Production By sector[d]				Total Arctic	Gross Domestic
Nation		1°	2°	3°	Other		
Canada	4,308	19	13	68	0	1.9	0.51
Denmark							
Faroe Islands	1,106	28	10	62	0	0.4	0.68
Greenland	1,003	8	29	63	0	0.5	0.71
Finland	12,201	7	27	63	3	5.3	9.63
Iceland	8,097	14	20	66	0	3.5	100.0
Norway	10,170	17	8	74	1	4.4	7.61
Sweden	11,045	19	6	74	1	4.8	5.14
Russian Federation	153,647	30	9	51	10	66.8	14.95
United States	28,581	22	6	70	0	12.4	0.29

[a] – Arctic region as illustrated in Figure 2.
[b] – Based on data from G Duhalme, 'Economic systems' in J N Larsen. (ed.), *Arctic Human Development Report*, Sustainable Development Working Group, Arctic Council (Akureyri, Stephansson Arctic Institute, 2004), pp. 69–84.
[c] – Standardised to 2001 US$.
[d] – 1° (precious minerals, fossil fuels and fisheries), 2° (manufacturing) and 3° (services).

year in 2007.[58] The Arctic economies further involve significant transfer of payments from regional and national governments to support human populations in the high north.

The largest Arctic economy by far is in Russia, which accounts for more than 66 per cent of the economic production in the high north – more than all other Arctic states combined (see Table 7). Other than Iceland, whose entire economy is limited within its island boundaries, Russia also has the largest Arctic contribution to its gross domestic product. Such productivity features, combined with the history and demographics of the region, provide baselines with which to interpret the economic consequences of climate-induced changes in the Arctic Ocean.

Changes in climate regulation from the Arctic Ocean, such as reduced albedo from the diminished sea ice, will also have economic consequences.[59] Such climate feedbacks have global ramifications.[60]

It is not yet a fait accompli that the Arctic Ocean will be ice-free during the boreal summer or that commercial activities can be safely, efficiently and reliably conducted in greatly thinned sea-ice conditions across the Arctic Ocean – but this transformation is underway. Engines are starting, competitors are lining up and the race is about to begin.[61] Assuming that the Arctic Ocean will be seasonally ice-free in three to five decades as predicted (Figure 3c), what will the maritime setting look like?

---

[58] United Nations Environmental Programme, 'Tourism in the Polar Regions: The Sustainability Challenge', 2007, <http://www.unepie.org/scp/publications/details.asp?id=DTI/0938/PA>.
[59] E Goodstein, E Euskirchen and H Huntington, *An Initial Estimate of the Cost of Lost Climate Regulation Services Due to Changes in the Arctic Cryosphere* (Washington, DC: Pew Charitable Trusts, 2010).
[60] N Stern, *The Economics of Climate Change: The Stern Review* (Cambridge: Cambridge University Press, 2007).
[61] R Howard, *The Arctic Gold Rush: The New Race for Tomorrow's Natural Resources* (London: Continuum, 2009).

Matters Of Security

Trade Route Implications of an Ice-Free Arctic Ocean
A seasonally ice-free Arctic Ocean will alter the dynamics of global trade, which throughout human history has shifted the balance of power.[62] Three routes through the Arctic Ocean are being considered (see Figure 9):

Figure 9: Shipping Routes in the Arctic Ocean through the Northwest Passage Adjacent to Canada, the Northeast Passage (or Northern Sea Route) Adjacent to Russia and Over the North Pole.[63]

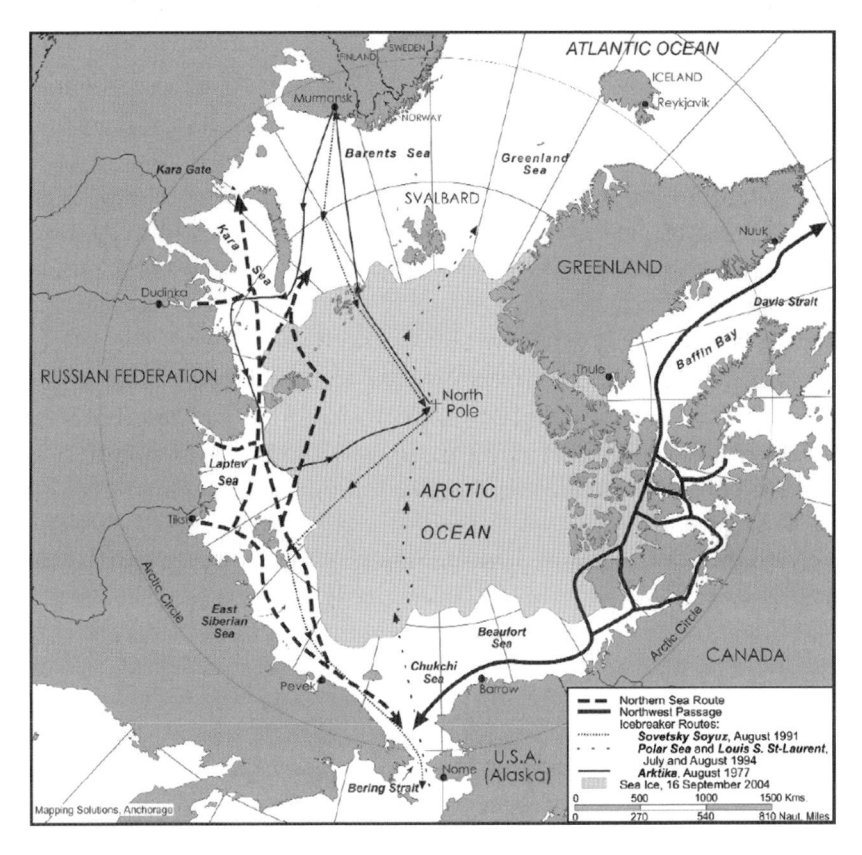

---

[62] D Held, A McGrew, D Goldblatt and J Perraton, *Global Transformations: Politics, Economics and Culture* (Stanford: Stanford University Press, 1999).

[63] L Brigham and B Ellis (eds), *Arctic Marine Transport Workshop,* Scott Polar Research Institute, Cambridge, 28–30 September 2004, <http://www.arctic.gov/publications/arctic_marine_transport.pdf>.

- Northeast Passage or Northern Sea Route along the coast of Russia
- Northwest Passage through the Canadian archipelago
- Across the centre of the Arctic Ocean over the North Pole.

Access to these routes will depend largely on the ice conditions, water depth and requirements of the Arctic coastal states. Projections indicate that sea ice will accumulate in the Northwest Passage while elsewhere in the Arctic Ocean remains ice-free, causing choke points for navigation.[64] First navigated by Roald Amundsen in 1906, corridors through the Northwest Passage are generally shallow, with only two of the five routes deep enough to allow transit by ships with a 20-metre draft.[65] Many of the routes through the Northeast Passage also are shallow, as in the Laptev and East Siberian Seas which have minimum depths of 6 and 13 metres respectively.[66]

In addition to the physical limitations of the Arctic coastal passages, there are legal requirements imposed by the adjacent coastal states, which have security implications.[67] For example, through the Canadian Arctic Waters Pollution Prevention Act, it is required that:[68]

> Canadian arctic [is] navigated only in a manner that takes cognizance of Canada's responsibility for the welfare of the Inuit and other inhabitants of the Canadian arctic and the preservation of the

---

[64] K J Wilson, J H Falkingham, H Melling and R De Abreu, 'Shipping in the Canadian Arctic: Other Possible Climate Change Scenarios' in *Proceedings of the IEEE International Geoscience and Remote Sensing Symposium*, Volume III (Piscataway, NJ: IEEE Press, 2004), pp. 1853–56, <http://www.arctic.noaa.gov/detect/KW_IGARSS04_NWP.pdf>.

[65] D Pharand and L H Legault, *International Straits of the World: Northwest Passage, Arctic Straits* (Boston: Martinus Nijhoff, 1984).

[66] N D Mulerin, 'The Northern Sea Route: Its Development and Evolving State of Operations in the 1990s', CRREL Report 96-3 (Alaska: Cold Regions Research and Engineering Laboratory, 1996).

[67] W Østreng (ed.), *National Security and International Environmental Cooperation in the Arctic: The Case of the Northern Sea Route* (Dordrecht, Kluwer Academic Publishers, 1999).

[68] Canadian Government, 'Arctic Waters Pollution Prevention Act', January 2010, <http://www.tc.gc.ca/media/documents/acts-regulations/A-12-acts.pdf>.

peculiar ecological balance that now exists in the water, ice and land areas of the Canadian arctic.

Similarly, the Northern Sea Route Administration of Russia has rules for vessel transit that include escorts by Russian icebreakers, designated routes and various fees.[69]

Between Europe and Asia, shipping through Arctic Ocean would offer routes that are 30 per cent shorter than current alternatives through the Panama or Suez Canals (Table 8).[70] Considered to be the first commercial transit across the Northeast Passage, the September 2009 voyages of the *Fraternity* and *Foresight* from Ulsan, South Korea, to Rotterdam, The Netherlands, are estimated to have saved the Beluga company $300,000 per ship and ten days transit compared to the 3,500-mile longer route through the Suez Canal.[71]

Table 8: Comparison of Ship Transit Distances through the Suez and Panama Canals versus the Northeast Passage across the Arctic Ocean.

	Suez Canal	**Panama Canal**	**Northeast Passage**
Rotterdam to Yokohama, Japan	12,894 miles	–	8,452 miles
Rotterdam to Shanghai, China	12,107 miles	–	9,297 miles
Rotterdam to Vancouver, Canada	–	10,262 miles	8,038 miles

Source: A C Kramer and A E Rivkin, 'Arctic Shortcut Beckons Shippers as Ice Thaws', *New York Times*, 11 September 2009.

Arctic Marine Shipping Assessment
As a baseline to interpret such shipping developments in the Arctic Ocean, the Arctic Council released the Arctic Marine Shipping Assessment (AMSA) in 2009.[72] The AMSA report, which was largely

---

[69] Arctic Operational Platform, 'Workshop 1: Legal and Administrative Issues', Helsinki, 2003.
[70] F Lasserre, 'High North Shipping: Myths and Realities' in S G Holtsmark and B A Smith-Windsor (eds), *Security Prospects in the High North: Geostrategic Thaw or Freeze?* (Rome: NATO Defense College, 2009).
[71] Adam, *op. cit.* in note 12.
[72] PAME, *op. cit.* in note 35.

based on 2004 data from each of the Arctic coastal states, revealed approximately 6,000 commercial vessels operating in the Arctic Ocean region. Locations of the vessels, however, were described within sovereign jurisdictions of the coastal states, which include areas of different dimensions in the North Atlantic and North Pacific south of the Arctic Circle. As mentioned above, for example, the Arctic shipping data from the United States included vessels in the Chuckchi Sea and around the Aleutian Islands. Moreover, the AMSA data was interpreted in relation to subsets of the Large Marine Ecosystem in the Arctic Ocean (Figure 6), which also have variable dimensions in a circumpolar context.

To interpret Arctic shipping trajectories over space in a consistent manner, the AMSA data was re-analysed just for the Arctic Ocean (as defined above) within 60° longitudinal sectors. This re-analysis indicates that about half of the vessels reported by AMSA were operating north of 66.5°N (Table 9). Similarly, compared to more than 515,000 fishing vessel days described in the AMSA report, there were about 350,000 fishing vessel days just north of the Arctic Circle (Table 9).

The largest number of vessels was in the Norwegian Sea/Barents Sea sector (0°–60°E) between Norway and Russia with the next largest concentration of ships in the Greenland Sea area (60°W–0°). There also were a relatively large number of ships in the Barents Sea (60°–120°E). Together, these data demonstrate that the predominance of maritime commercial vessel traffic in the Arctic Ocean is currently travelling to and from the North Atlantic. This conclusion is further supported by AMSA data for the fishing vessels, which was only reported from the Atlantic side of the Arctic Ocean.

On the Pacific Ocean side, traffic runs through the Bering Strait between the United States and Russia, and the largest number of ships was reported in the Beaufort Sea (180°–60°W). Compared to the North Atlantic (Figures 1, 5 and 9), the connection to the North Pacific through the Bering Strait is relatively constricted and may be a potential choke point for future vessel traffic through the Arctic Ocean; certainly this is an area in which to promote co-operation and prevent conflict between the United States and Russian Federation.

Passenger ships associated with tourism accounted for the largest number of vessels in the Arctic Ocean in 2004. Ships

Table 9: Arctic Ocean Shipping North of the Arctic Circle (66.5°N) in 2004.[a]

Shipping vessel type	0°–60°e	60°–120°e	120°–180°e	180°–120°w	120°–60°w	60°w–0°	Total
Number of unique vessel journeys in each longitudinal sector							
Bulk Carrier	446	42	3	23	2	11	**527**
General Cargo Ship	473	37	13	13	11	31	**578**
Container Ship	29	29	0	0	0	50	**108**
Tanker Ship	206	25	9	4	10	35	**289**
Tug/Barge	22	0	0	288	5	0	**315**
Passenger Ship	223	0	0	5	27	599	**854**
Government Vessel	51	95	9	14	8	72	**249**
TOTAL	**1,504**	**228**	**34**	**347**	**63**	**798**	**2,974**
Number of Shipping Vessel Days in Each Longitudinal Sector							
Fishing Vessel	200,884	115,784	0	0	21,397	212,738	349,919

[a] Data from PAME, *op. cit.* in note 35, which included information south of the Arctic Circle, has been re-analysed for shipping north of 66.5°N (Figure 1); re-analysis performed by William Eucker (unpublished). The Norwegian data is from 2006 and all other data is from 2004.

associated with commerce (bulk carrier, cargo, container ships and tug/barge) accounted for nearly half of the ships in the Arctic Ocean. However, this data introduces subjective features because it applies to the functions of the vessels rather than their dimensions, which would be unambiguous. To interpret Arctic shipping trajectories over time in a consistent manner, the AMSA data could be re-analysed based on ship sizes (for instance tonnage and length). Such analyses could be used to assess how Arctic shipping varies within and between years in relation to sea-ice extent. Moreover, for the real-time basis required for operational decisions, satellite data could provide a framework for circumpolar observations that would remove the variability of reporting by individual states.

Government vessels were also inconsistently accounted by the Arctic coastal states in the 2009 AMSA report, but did include ships associated with surveying, oceanographic research, vessel escort in ice, salvage, pollution response and search and rescue. However, 'in keeping with the scope of the Arctic Council, naval or military vessels were not included in the AMSA database'.[73] Looking ahead, presumably with trillion-dollar opportunities[74] of trade routes opening up in the Arctic Ocean:[75]

> The infrastructure required to support such shipping may include port facilities, search and rescue or emergency response capability, and mechanisms of governance or enforcement, which may include military presence to preserve sovereign claims over certain waters.

International Maritime Co-operation

The assertion of military assets to preserve sovereign claims would be a source of potential instability in the Arctic Ocean which requires shared dialogue to avoid. Currently, Arctic coastal states are peacefully addressing jurisdictional disagreements. For example, negotiations that have been ongoing over the past forty years between Russia and Norway regarding a disputed region of the

---

[73] PAME, *op. cit.* in note 35.
[74] M Stopford, *Maritime Economics*, 3rd edition (New York: Routledge, 2009).
[75] PAME, *op. cit.* in note 35.

Barents Sea were concluded in April 2010 without the use of military force.[76]

Similarly, Canada and the United States reached the 1988 Agreement on Arctic Cooperation[77] that relates to transit through the Canadian archipelago:

> The Government of the United States pledges that all navigation by U.S. icebreakers within waters claimed by Canada to be internal will be undertaken with the consent of the Government of Canada.

Basically, this agreement indicates that the United States would not send icebreakers through the Northwest Passage without Canada's consent, and Canada would always give that consent. The wider issue of rights of innocent passage or transit passage under the law of the sea[78] remain unresolved, despite the fact that the transportation of resources through the Northwest Passage to 'markets of the world [is] of potentially great significance to international trade and commerce', as described in Canada's Arctic Waters Pollution Prevention Act.[79] Referring to the four pillars of Canada's Arctic Foreign Policy in August 2010, Foreign Minister Lawrence Cannon reiterated that 'making progress on outstanding boundary issues will be a top priority.'[80]

Co-ordinated naval and coastguard co-operation among all Arctic coastal states will be fundamental to safety-of-life at sea, emergency response, environmental protection, fisheries conservation and other activities to ensure sustainable development in the Arctic Ocean.[81] One avenue to promote

---

[76] *BBC News*, 'Norway Agrees Barents Sea Arctic Border with Russia', 27 April 2010.

[77] Agreement on Arctic Cooperation Between Canada and the United States, Ottawa, 11 January 1988, <http://untreaty.un.org/unts/60001_120000/30/4/00058175.pdf>.

[78] EvREsearch Ltd, *op. cit.*

[79] Canadian Government, *op. cit.*

[80] Address by Minister Cannon at Launch of Statement on Canada's Arctic Foreign Policy, 20 August 2010, Ottawa, Ontario, Canada <http://www.international.gc.ca/media/aff/speeches-discours/2010/2010-057.aspx?lang=eng>.

[81] Holtsmark and Smith-Windsor, *op. cit.*

such co-operation, as well as to prevent conflict in the Arctic Ocean, may be the North Atlantic Coast Guard Forum (Table 3), which was established in 2007 with all eight Arctic states and twelve non-Arctic states:[82]

> to facilitate multilateral cooperation on matters related to combined operations, illegal drug trafficking, marine security, environmental protection, information exchange, fisheries enforcement, illegal migration and search and rescue. The NACGF may also provide a forum for the exchange of technical experiences including but not limited to maritime surveillance systems, equipment and shipbuilding.

There also are urgent issues of ship design to be considered in order to minimise the risk of accidents that could cause loss of life at sea or pollute Arctic marine ecosystems. The risks of navigating the polar regions has been well known since the 1912 sinking of the *Titanic*, which stimulated the first version of the International Convention for the Safety of Life at Sea in 1914.[83] The risks of polar navigation still exist, as reflected by the Antarctic sinking of the M/S *Explorer* in 2007 with more than 150 passengers onboard, all of whom fortunately survived.[84]

Resource Exploitation: Fisheries and Fossil Fuels
In addition to commercial or passenger transport, increased shipping will involve risks to marine ecosystems from expanding fisheries as the sea ice retreats and new opportunities to exploit living resources appear in the Arctic Ocean. There will also be various risks of conflict associated with illegal, unreported or

---

[82] North Atlantic Coast Guard Forum, <http://www.ccg-gcc.gc.ca/e0003559>.

[83] Versions of the International Convention for the Safety of Life at Sea from 1914 to the present are available at <http://www.imo.org/InfoResource/mainframe.asp?topic_id=904&doc_id=4842#17b>.

[84] *BBC News*, 'Stricken Antarctic Ship Evacuated', 24 November 2008.

unregulated fishing.[85] However, at this stage, as concluded by the Arctic Transform project:[86]

> For most of the Arctic Ocean, the presence of ice-cover for most if not all of the year has inhibited research on fish stocks and related species. Accordingly, relatively little baseline data exists with respect to these living marine resources, nor is much known about the changes in their composition that may be occurring, particularly in the central portion of the Arctic Ocean. There has been little research conducted on the potential effects of commercial fishing on these resources and on Arctic marine ecosystem(s) as a whole.

While Arctic shipping routes may revolutionise international trade (Figure 9, Table 9) and while there may be increased fisheries in a seasonally ice-free Arctic Ocean, of all the commercial activities, 'energy is the crucial factor in the planet's economic development'.[87] Energy interests in the Arctic are long-standing:[88]

> Since the 1970s, Arctic regions of the Unites States (Alaska), Canada, Norway and, in particular, Russia have been producing large volumes of both oil and (with the exception of Alaska) gas.

Moreover, with rising global demand, oil and gas activity in the Arctic region is expected to increase.[89] The issues of potential energy supplies in the Arctic Ocean are significant on a global scale, and in 2009 the United States Geological Survey 'assessed the area north of the Arctic Circle and concluded that about 30

---

[85] FAO Fisheries and Aquaculture Department, 'Illegal, Unreported and Unregulated (IUU) Fishing', <http://www.fao.org/fishery/topic/3195/en>, accessed 5 August 2010.
[86] Arctic Transform, 'Policy Options for Arctic Environmental Governance', Fisheries Working Group Policy Paper, March 2009, <http://arctic-transform.org/download/FishEX.pdf>.
[87] G8 Energy Ministers' Meeting 2009, <http://www.g8italia2009.it/G8/Home/IncontriMinisteriali/G8-G8_Layout_locale-1199882116809_MinisterialeEnergia.htm>.
[88] AMAP, 'Arctic Oil and Gas Assessment 2007' (Oslo: AMAP, 2008).
[89] *Ibid*.

per cent of the world's undiscovered gas and 13 per cent of the world's undiscovered oil may be found there'.[90]

The Arctic may contain about 618 billion barrels of oil and, on an energy-equivalent basis, more than three times as much undiscovered gas with a high probability (greater than 95 per cent chance) that more than 770 trillion cubic feet of gas occurs north of the Arctic Circle.[91] Considering their global significance – as well as potential impacts to associated ecosystems, environments and human populations – energy resource activities have great potential to influence political, cultural and economic instability in the Arctic Ocean region.

As noted in the briefing paper for the NATO meeting in advance of the 30 January 2009 meeting in Reykjavik, Iceland: 'Long-term security challenges in the High North are linked to the prospect and effects of climate change and the potential significance of still-unexplored Arctic petroleum resources'.[92] With increasing access to the Arctic Ocean, questions about hydrocarbon resources have escalated into more pronounced assertions about national interests in the Arctic Ocean, both within accepted boundaries and across jurisdictional extensions proposed to the Commission on the Limits of the Continental Shelf.

It is largely because of potential mineral resources that the 2007 Russian flag planting has become the rallying cry of the five coastal states for their 'sovereignty, sovereign rights and jurisdiction in large areas of the Arctic Ocean' – collectively stated in the May 2008 Ilulissat Declaration.[93] Independently, the United States declared its 'sovereignty, sovereign rights, and jurisdiction in the Arctic region' in the January 2009 Arctic Region Policy.[94]

---

[90] D L Gautier, K J Bird, R R Charpentier, A Grantz, D W Houseknecht, T R Klett, T E Moore, J K Pitman, C J Schenk, J H Schuenemeyer, K Sørensen, M E Tennyson, Z C Valin and C J Wandrey, 'Assessment of Undiscovered Oil and Gas in the Arctic', *Science* (Vol. 234, 2009), pp. 175–79.
[91] *Ibid.*
[92] S G Holtsmark, 'Cooperation Rather than Confrontation: Security in the High North', NATO Research Briefing (Rome: NATO Defense College, 2009).
[93] Ilulissat Declaration, *op. cit.*
[94] United States National Security Presidential Directive 66, 'Arctic Region Policy', 9 January 2009.

Matters Of Security

Similarly, the March 2009 state policy of the Russian Federation discusses its 'sovereign rights and jurisdiction under international law' in the Arctic Ocean.[95]

Non-Arctic nations are seeking an enhanced role in the Arctic Council (Table 3) to more actively contribute to the multilateral discussions about 'common Arctic issues' with the Arctic nations and indigenous peoples organisations. The European Parliament approved a resolution on Arctic Governance in October 2008.[96] In November 2008, the European Commission adopted a Communication on the European Union and the Arctic Region,[97] paving the way for the European Council Conclusions on Arctic Issues in December 2009.[98]

International interests cannot be brushed aside when it comes to future resource activities in the Arctic Ocean. The corollary is that stewardship, as mentioned in the 2008 Ilulissat Declaration,[99] involves accommodation among Arctic and non-Arctic states (Table 3) as well as indigenous peoples. As an analogue, international responses to Antarctic mineral resources starting in the mid-1970s are instructive (Figure 10).

In 1973/74, the world was faced with the OPEC oil embargo.[100] While drilling in the Ross Sea floor to interpret the

---

[95] 'Basics of the State Policy of the Russian Federation in the Arctic for the Period until 2020 and for a Further Perspective', 18 September 2008 in *Rossiyskaya Gazeta,* 30 March 2009, translated by Boris Shapovalov, <http://www.arcticgovernance.org/russia-basics-of-the-state-policy-of-the-russian-federation-in-the-arctic-for-the-period-till-2020-and-for-a-further-perspective.4651232-142902.html>.

[96] European Union, 'European Parliament Resolution on Arctic Governance', 9 October 2008.

[97] Communication from the Commission to the European Parliament and the Council, 'The European Union and the Arctic Region', 20 November 2008.

[98] Council of the European Union, 'Council Conclusions on Arctic Issues', 8 December 2009, <http://www.consilium.europa.eu/ueDocs/cms_Data/docs/pressData/EN/foraff/111814.pdf>.

[99] Ilulissat Declaration, *op. cit.*

[100] D Yergin, *The Prize: The Epic Quest for Oil, Money, and Power* (New York: Simon & Schuster, 1993).

sedimentary history of Antarctic glaciation, the Glomar Challenger also uncovered petroleum residues. Within months, it was reported that the Antarctic continental shelf might 'contain up to 45 billion barrels of oil and 115 trillion cubic feet of natural gas'.[101]

Figure 10: Phases of International Development Involving Spaces beyond Sovereign Jurisdictions.[102]

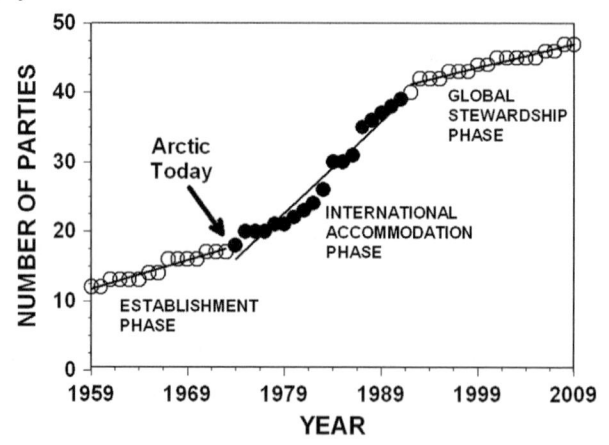

Note: Data is based on the accession of nations to the 1959 Antarctic Treaty during its first fifty years,[103] with statistically different regression lines for each phase. The average annual entrance rate of nations into the Antarctic Treaty System accelerated nearly 500 per cent in the mid-1970s following estimates of billions of barrels of oil and trillions of cubic feet of natural gas on the Antarctic continental shelf, which are the same order of magnitude as estimates in the Arctic Ocean today. International engagement in the Arctic is just at the inflection point (arrow) between the establishment phase and accomodation phase.

---

[101] N A Wright and P L Williams, 'Mineral Resources of Antarctica: Geological Survey Circular 705' (Reston: United States Geological Survey, 1974).
[102] Berkman, *op. cit.* Also see Tables 5 and 6.
[103] See the Antarctic Treaty Secretariat, and the 'Antarctic Treaty Summit: Science-Policy Interactions in International Governance' convened to assess global lessons from Antarctica on the 50th anniversary of the Antarctic Treaty, <http://www.atsummit50.aq>.

Public speculation about the mineral resource potential of Antarctica dramatically shifted international attention southward.

During the establishment phase of the Antarctic Treaty System (ATS) from 1961 to 1976, on average less than one new nation acceded to the Antarctic Treaty every two years.[104] However, with the onset of speculation about abundant mineral resources, the annual entrance rate of nations into the ATS skyrocketed over 500 per cent. Coinciding with the adoption of the Protocol on Environmental Protection to the Antarctic Treaty in 1991, the entrance of new nations suddenly levelled as the ATS began shifting into a 'global stewardship phase'. Speculation that '30 per cent of the world's undiscovered oil and 13 per cent of the world's undiscovered gas' – with hydrocarbon volumes that are the same orders of magnitude as those that compelled the international accommodation in Antarctica – suggests that the Arctic is poised just at the inflection between the establishment and international accommodation phases that precede global stewardship (see Figure 10).

Current discussions about economics in the Arctic Ocean emphasise commercial opportunities, asking questions such as: What is needed so that 'Arctic routes can be safe, efficient, reliable and economically viable'[105] for shipping? How can the Arctic coastal states protect 'their sovereignty, sovereign rights and jurisdiction in large areas of the Arctic Ocean'[106] for the potential exploitation of natural resources? Recognising that the Arctic Council lacks 'decision making authority and material resources'[107] – even with its working group on Emergency, Prevention, Preparedness and Response – the International Maritime Organisation (IMO) and its associated institutions will be increasingly tasked to ensure safe, secure and reliable shipping in the Arctic Ocean. The regulatory slate is not

---

[104] Antarctic Treaty Secretariat, 'Antarctic Treaty Parties', <http://www.ats.aq/devAS/ats_parties.aspx?lang=e>, accessed 5 August 2010.

[105] PAME, *op. cit.*

[106] Ilulissat Declaration, *op. cit.*

[107] O R Young, 'Whither the Arctic? Conflict or Cooperation in the Circumpolar North', *Polar Record* (Vol. 45, 2009), pp. 73–82.

entirely blank: the IMO did publish 'Guidelines for Ships Operating in Ice-covered Arctic Waters' that were adopted in 2002.[108] However, these guidelines are only voluntary and the Arctic Council has urged:[109]

> [The] IMO to update the Guidelines for Ships Operating in Arctic Ice-Covered Waters ... application of its relevant parts be made mandatory, and global IMO ship safety and pollution prevention conventions be augmented with specific mandatory requirements or other provisions for ship construction, design, equipment, crewing, training, and operations, aimed at safety and protection of the Arctic environment.

However, underlying dialogue about economic opportunities are questions that involve militaries in the Arctic Ocean (for example, Figure 8). How can naval and coastguard assets be co-ordinated 'to facilitate multilateral cooperation on matters related to combined operations'[110] in the Arctic Ocean? Beyond the bluff and bluster, the question needs to be asked about what the real risks, flashpoints and tell-tale signs of militarisation are among the Arctic coastal states to preserve their economic opportunities in the Arctic Ocean. As noted in a 2009 memorandum from the US Department of the Navy:[111]

> This opening of the Arctic may lead to increased resource development, research, tourism, and could reshape the global transportation system. These developments offer opportunities for growth, but also are potential sources of competition and conflict for access and natural resources. Reducing the uncertainties in these projections will enable the Navy to make better-informed investment and policy decisions. This is a key objective of this roadmap.

Economic activities are important drivers of stability as well as potential instability in the Arctic Ocean that

---

[108] IMO, 'Guidelines for Ships Operating In Arctic Ice-Covered Waters' (London: International Maritime Organization, 2002).
[109] Tromsø Declaration, *op. cit.*
[110] North Atlantic Coast Guard Forum, <http://www.ccg-gcc.gc.ca/e0003559>.
[111] Admiral J W Greenert, Vice Chief of Naval Operations, *Navy Artic Roadmap* (Washington, DC: Department of the Navy, 2009).

require shared dialogue and stewardship from all of the Arctic coastal states, in particular, to promote co-operation and prevent conflict in this globally relevant region.

Cultural Stability

The Arctic Ocean is associated with varied cultures. Surrounding the Arctic Ocean are the indigenous peoples who have inhabited the region for millennia and immigrants who largely settled in the region during the twentieth century (Figure 2). There also are cultural dimensions associated with human activities in the Arctic Ocean (for instance, Figure 8). **With the environmental state-change in the Arctic Ocean (Figure 3), the cultural challenge is to assess direct and indirect impacts on the attitudes, values, goals, and practices of the dependent groups.**

The 2004 Arctic Human Development Report provides a diverse assessment of the circumstances and trends of human populations in the Arctic.[112] On the one hand, it has been suggested that:[113]

> Arctic societies and cultures are highly adaptable and resilient and thus well-equipped for integrating change. The fact that they integrate modernity should be viewed positively rather than with nostalgia for traditions lost. The concept of traditions should be seen as a dynamic one: traditions do not and should not hinder development.

The same author also notes, however, that:[114]

> Among indigenous peoples, recent changes have been so precipitous that they have been interpreted by outsiders as a break from the past, and in some cases even, as a breakdown of societies and cultures. In particular, transformations have been associated with major communication gaps between generations.

The 'communication gaps between generations' are reflected most seriously in the decline and even loss of native

---

[112] *Arctic Human Development Report, op. cit.*
[113] Y Csonka and P Schweitzer in *Arctic Human Development Report, op. cit.*, pp. 45–68.
[114] *Ibid.*

languages, following their replacement by languages that originated outside of the Arctic (Russian, English, Norwegian, Icelandic, Swedish and Finnish, in order of dominance).[115] There is also a declining transfer of indigenous knowledge through cultural expressions of songs, dances and other art forms. A sad consequence of lost cultural identity is revealed in some Arctic areas by suicide rates among young indigenous peoples (15–24 years) that are nearly twice as high as non-indigenous peoples.[116]

While indigenous peoples have demonstrated resilience in the face of environmental and ecosystem changes over the millennia, since the mid-twentieth century they have been increasingly tasked with responding to economic, legal and political systems superimposed on them.[117] There has been some integration of indigenous peoples into the 'Resource Frontier'[118] economies that are developing in the Arctic. One notable example is the Alaskan Red Dog Mine, which is the largest producer of zinc concentrate in the world.[119] In this case, there is benefit-sharing between the mine operator (Cominco) and the Northwest Alaska Native Association[120] that was formed in connection with the 1971 Alaska Native Claims Settlement Act,[121] which itself represents a successful legal and political outcome as the largest single indigenous peoples claims settlement in the history of the United States.

---

[115] *Ibid.*

[116] C M Hild, V Stordahl, P Bjerregaard, T Tine Curtis, R V Kalstad, R Kemi, R Koposov, B Saylor, A R Spein and R Wells, 'Human Health and Well Being' in *Arctic Human Development Report, op. cit.*

[117] B S Zellen, *On Thin Ice: The Inuit, the State and the Challenge of Arctic Sovereignty* (New York: Lexington Books, 2009).

[118] Sugden, *op. cit.*

[119] G Duhaime, A Lemelin, V Didyk, O Goldsmith, G Winther, A Andrée Caron, N Bernard and A Godmaire, 'Economic Systems' in *Arctic Human Development Report, op. cit.*

[120] NANA Regional Corporation, <http://www.nana.com/>.

[121] Alaska Native Claims Settlement Act Resource Center, <http://www.lbblawyers.com/ancsa.htm>.

Matters Of Security

Other indigenous rights' developments have occurred in the territories of Canada, such as Nunavat,[122] the Home Rule government in Greenland,[123] Sámi Parliaments in Finland,[124] Norway[125] and Sweden,[126] and through the organisations that are permanent participants of the Arctic Council.[127] As former Greenland Home Rule Premier Jonathan Motzfeldt stated in 1999:[128]

> things were administered by Danes, decisions were taken by Danes, and problems were solved by Danes ... The common Greenlander had a feeling of standing outside, of being observer of an enormous development, which s/he did not have the necessary background to understand.

In a circumpolar context – recognising that 'international relations must give primary respect to the need for global environmental security' – Arctic indigenous peoples have declared that:[129]

> The conduct of international relations in the Arctic and the resolution of international disputes in the Arctic are not the sole preserve of Arctic states or other states; they are also within the purview of the Arctic's indigenous peoples ... Issues of sovereignty and sovereign rights in the Arctic have become inextricably linked to issues of self-determination in the Arctic.

This statement from the 2009 Circumpolar Inuit Declaration on Arctic Sovereignty is complemented on a global scale by the 2007 United Nations Declaration on the Rights of Indigenous

---

[122] <http://www.gov.nu.ca/English/>.
[123] <http://www.nanoq.gl/>.
[124] <http://www.samediggi.fi/index.php?lang=fi>.
[125] <http://www.samediggi.no/artikkel.aspx?AId=3539&MId1=3376&back=1>.
[126] <http://www.sametinget.se/>.
[127] <http://arctic-council.org/section/permanent_participants>.
[128] J Motzfeldt, 'Forord' in B Gynther and M Aqigssiaq (eds), *Kalaallit Nunaat: Gyldendals bog om Grønland*, Gyldendalske Boghandel (Copenhagen: Nordisk Forlag A/S, 1999), p. 7.
[129] Circumpolar Inuit Declaration on Arctic Sovereignty, April 2009, <http://www.itk.ca/circumpolar-inuit-declaration-arctic-sovereignty>.

Peoples.[130] **Even with their growing political, economic and legal capacity, it is likely that the cultural dilution of indigenous peoples will continue with expanding economic activity and population encroachment around the Arctic Ocean.**

In addition to the cultures of the peoples (Figure 2), there are cultural dimensions of the activities that are dependent on the Arctic Ocean. In particular, there is the concept of a military culture,[131] which certainly resonates with the extensive and long-standing naval presence in the Arctic Ocean (for instance, see Figure 8).

Russia's Northern Fleet is one of the world's great naval forces, deeply rooted in the culture of the Russian Federation as an important tool of foreign policy.[132] Moreover, emergent economic activities of the Russian Federation in the Arctic Ocean are themselves seen through the lens of the Northern Fleet.[133]

In the United States, there have been active discussions since 2001 to examine naval operations, requirements and policies in an ice-diminished Arctic Ocean, where '[e]nsuring access and stabilizing the global commons are the most overriding reasons for increased operations in the Arctic'.[134] Further considering the impact of an ice-diminishing Arctic on naval and maritime operations in 2007, it was observed that '[t]he U.S. and other countries are working in the Arctic

---

[130] United Nations, Declaration on the Rights of Indigenous Peoples, General Assembly Resolution 61/295, 13 September 2007, <http://www.un.org/esa/socdev/unpfii/documents/DRIPS_en.pdf>.

[131] A D English, *Understanding Military Culture: A Canadian Perspective* (Montreal: McGill-Queen's University Press, 2004).

[132] K Zysk, 'Russia's Arctic Strategy: Ambitions and Constraints', *Joint Forces Quarterly* (Vol. 57, No. 2, 2010), pp. 103–10.

[133] K Åtland, 'Russia's Northern Fleet and the Oil Industry—Rivals or Partners? Petroleum, Security, and Civil–Military Relations in the Post-Cold War European Arctic', *Armed Forces and Society* (Vol. 35, 2009), pp. 362–84.

[134] Office of Naval Research, 'Final Report: Naval Operations in an Ice-free Arctic Symposium', Washington, DC, 17–21 April 2001, <http://www.natice.noaa.gov/icefree/finalarcticreport.pdf>.

now – northern peoples are being impacted now. This is not a discussion that can wait for the future – the future is upon us.'[135]

Clearly, there is growing recognition of the 'new strategic significance' of the Arctic Ocean as 'a region where security, economics and the environment interact'.[136] **Stability of the military culture in the Arctic Ocean is a central issue for shared dialogue that underlies all other decisions about responding to the environmental state-change in the Arctic Ocean.**

---

[135] National Ice Center, 'Impact of an Ice-Diminishing Arctic on Naval and Maritime Operations', Washington, DC, 10–12 July 2007, <http://www.star.nesdis.noaa.gov/star/documents/2007IceSymp/Summary_Report_2007.pdf>.

[136] M Blunden, 'The New Problem of Arctic Stability', *Survival* (Vol. 5, No. 5, 2009), pp. 121–42.

5. ARCTIC OCEAN STEWARDSHIP

Institutional Interplay

While the context of 'sovereignty, sovereign rights and jurisdictions' was emphasised by the five Arctic coastal states in the 2008 Ilulissat Declaration, they also identified the Arctic Ocean as 'a unique ecosystem, which the five coastal states have a stewardship role in protecting'.[1] This 'stewardship role' is a shared statement about the central responsibilities of the five Arctic coastal states to manage human activities in the Arctic Ocean. **However, Arctic Ocean stewardship is in the interests of all humankind, with vision decades to centuries into the future.** Such stewardship carries with it an obligation to address the 'institutional interplay'[2] of rights and responsibilities in the Arctic Ocean.

Commitment to UNCLOS

As a starting point, the Arctic coastal states collectively demonstrated their stewardship through the 2008 Ilulissat Declaration by acknowledging that they 'remain committed' to the 'law of the sea' as the umbrella legal framework for managing human activities in the Arctic Ocean.[3] The law of the sea is taken to

---

[1] The Ilulissat Declaration from the Arctic Ocean Conference, Ilulissat, Greenland, 28 May 2008, <http://www.oceanlaw.org/downloads/arctic/Ilulissat_Declaration.pdf>.

[2] O R Young, 'Institutional Interplay: The Environmental Consequences of Cross-Scale Interactions' in E Ostrom (ed.), *The Drama of the Commons* (Washington, DC: National Academy Press, 2002).

[3] Ilulissat Declaration, *op. cit.*

Figure 11: Concentric Levels of Responsibilities to Manage Human Activities in the Arctic Ocean.

Note: The five Arctic coastal states, three Arctic non-coastal states (Table 2) and six indigenous peoples organisations were the original signatories to the 1996 Ottawa Declaration that established the Arctic Council.[4] Additional involvement of non-Arctic states in Arctic organisations (Table 3) and engagement non-state actors, especially industry, reflects the interplay of global civil society in the Arctic Ocean.

be the 1982 United Nations Convention on the Law of the Sea (UNCLOS), in force for all the Arctic states – with the exception of the United States, which has yet to ratify – and more than 155 nations (Table 2). 'With due regard for the sovereignty of all States', UNCLOS provides:[5]

> a legal order for the seas and oceans which will facilitate international communication, and will promote the peaceful uses of the seas and oceans, the equitable and efficient utilization of their resources, the conservation of their living resources, and the study, protection and preservation of the marine environment.

---

[4] Declaration on the Establishment of the Arctic Council, Ottawa, 19 September 1996.
[5] EvREsearch Ltd, 'Law of the Sea Searchable Database', <http://lawofthesea.tierit.com>.

National policies further reveal individual commitments of the Arctic coastal states to the law of the sea:[6]

> As reality changes in the Arctic Ocean, we are fortunate to already have in place a robust framework of international law. In particular the international Law of the Sea provides the necessary framework to ensure responsible management of the Arctic Ocean and its resources.

For example, the United States and Russian Federation each adopted policies in 2009 regarding their sovereignty, sovereign rights and jurisdiction over the territorial sea, contiguous zone, exclusive economic zone (EEZ) and continental shelf emanating from their respective coastal boundaries.[7] However, these national policies are without reference to the international sea zones beyond sovereign jurisdictions (Table 5), namely the high seas beyond the EEZ and the area of the deep sea beyond the continental shelf. The lasting value of UNCLOS is its international and inclusive framework that considers the rights and responsibilities of all nations with regard to all ocean areas across the Earth, including the Arctic Ocean (Figure 12).

Progressing seaward from the coastal baselines, there is a gradient from national to international jurisdictions (Figure 12).[8] As stated in UNCLOS Article 56, beyond the twelve-mile territorial sea and contiguous zone (out to a distance of 200 nautical miles) is the EEZ, where the coastal state has:[9]

> sovereign rights for the purpose of exploring and exploiting, conserving and managing the natural resources, whether living or

---

[6] J G Støre, 'Perspectives on the Arctic and Norway's High North Policy', Arctic Frontiers Conference, Tromsø, 19 January 2009 (presented by E Walaas).
[7] United States National Security Presidential Directive 66, 'Arctic Region Policy', 9 January 2009; 'Basics of the State Policy of the Russian Federation in the Arctic for the Period until 2020 and for a Further Perspective', 18 September 2008 in *Rossiyskaya Gazeta*, 30 March 2009, translated by Boris Shapovalov, <http://www.arcticgovernance.org/russia-basics-of-the-state-policy-of-the-russian-federation-in-the-arctic-for-the-period-till-2020-and-for-a-further-perspective.4651232-142902.html>.
[8] P A Berkman, 'Arctic Ocean State-Changes: Self Interests and Common Interests', Polar Law Symposium, Akureryi, Iceland, 2009.
[9] EvREsearch Ltd, *op. cit.*

Figure 12: Zones throughout the World Ocean,[10] from the Coastal Boundaries of Nation-States into the International Spaces beyond Sovereign Jurisdictions.

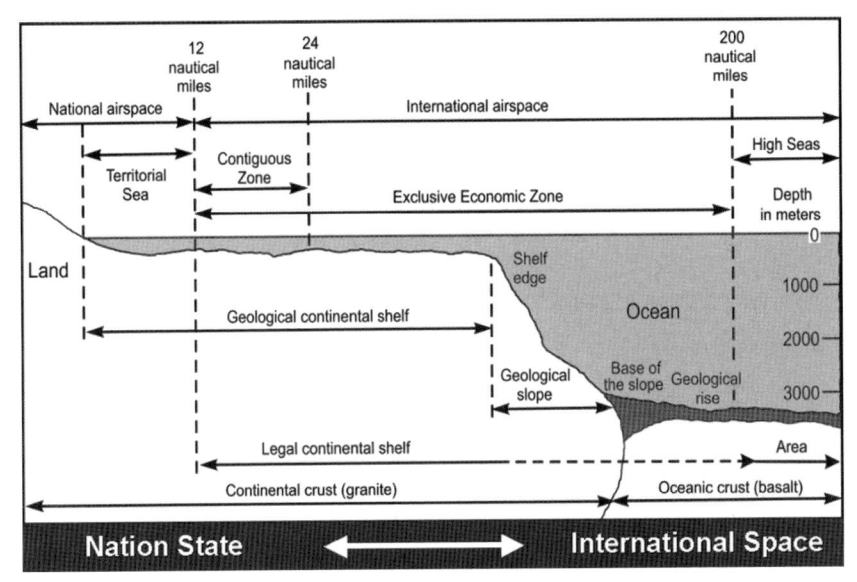

Note: The zones (territorial sea, contiguous zone, EEZ, high seas, continental shelf, area, national airspace and international air space are defined by customary international law and the 1982 UNCLOS[11] with provisions that 'will contribute to the strengthening of peace, security, co-operation and friendly relations among all nations'.[12]

> non-living, of the waters superjacent to the sea-bed and of the sea-bed and its subsoil, and with regard to other activities for the economic exploitation and exploration of the zone, such as the production of energy from the water, currents and winds.

Moreover, as stated in UNCLOS Article 234 with regard to ice-covered areas:

---

[10] Adapted, with addition of 'area', from: United States Department of State, *Third Conference on the United Nations Convention on the Law of the Sea* (Washington, DC: Government Printing Office, 1985).
[11] United Nations Convention on the Law of the Sea, Montego Bay, Jamaica, 10 December 1982, entry into force 16 November 1994, <http://www.un.org/Depts/los/convention_agreements/convention_overview_convention.htm>.
[12] EvREsearch Ltd, *op. cit.*

Coastal States have the right to adopt and enforce non-discriminatory laws and regulations for the prevention, reduction and control of marine pollution from vessels in ice-covered areas within the limits of the exclusive economic zone.

Beyond the EEZ are the high seas. Generally, underneath the high seas is the 'area', which is the international space of the deep sea (Table 5). In some locations, however, the high seas may also overlie the continental shelf. Indeed, following recommendations of the Commission on the Limits of the Continental Shelf,[13] as instituted under UNCLOS Article 76, Norway has already been shown to have a continental shelf that extends beyond 200 nautical miles into the Arctic Ocean.[14] Additional submissions to the Commission on the Limits of the Continental Shelf are pending from the Russian Federation (2001),[15] Denmark (2009)[16] and Iceland (2009).[17] Nonetheless, the high seas exist in the superjacent waters, legally and ecologically distinct from the sea floor, whether the area or continental shelf. **In the centre of the Arctic Ocean, the high seas will remain an unambiguous and undisputed international space (Tables 5 and 6).**

---

[13] Commission on the Limits of the Continental Shelf, <http://www.un.org/Depts/los/clcs_new/clcs_home.htm>.

[14] Commission on the Limits of the Continental Shelf, 'Summary of the Recommendations of the Commission on the Limits of the Continental Shelf in Regard to the Submission Made by Norway in Respect of Areas in the Arctic Ocean, the Barents Sea and the Norwegian Sea on 27 November 2006', 27 March 2009, <http://www.un.org/Depts/los/clcs_new/submissions_files/nor06/nor_rec_summ.pdf>.

[15] Submission from the Russian Federation to the Commission on the Limits of the Continental Shelf, <http://www.un.org/Depts/los/clcs_new/submissions_files/submission_rus.htm>.

[16] Submission from Denmark to the Commission on the Limits of the Continental Shelf, <http://www.un.org/Depts/los/clcs_new/submissions_files/submission_dnk_28_2009.htm>.

[17] Submission from the Republic of Iceland to the Commission on the Limits of the Continental Shelf, <http://www.un.org/Depts/los/clcs_new/submissions_files/submission_isl_27_2009.htm>.

In light of the interplay of actors and responsibilities (Figure 11), discussions that have occurred between the five Arctic coastal states only – such as the 28 May 2008 meeting in Ilulissat, Greenland, and the 29 March 2010 meeting in Chelsea, Quebec – have led to concerns about the full engagement of the three other Arctic states and indigenous peoples organisations who shared in the development of the Arctic Council. This concern was acknowledged by US Secretary of State Hillary Clinton at the recent Chelsea meeting:[18]

> Significant international discussions on Arctic issues should include those who have legitimate interests in the region. And I hope the Arctic will always showcase our ability to work together, not create new divisions.

There is long-standing involvement of non-Arctic states in Arctic matters (Table 3), as illustrated by the 1920 Treaty Concerning the Archipelago of Spitsbergen, which established an 'equitable regime, in order to assure their development and peaceful utilization ... which may never be used for warlike purposes'.[19] By the time that the Spitsbergen Treaty came into force, there were twenty-three signatories, including all of the Arctic states except Russia (which acceded in 1935) and Iceland (which was the most recent to accede in 1994). Today, there are forty-two parties to the Spitsbergen Treaty, involving states from every continent that contains indigenous human populations. The Spitsbergen Treaty reflects the interest of the global community in preventing conflict in the Arctic Ocean, both in its participation and its conceptual design.

More recently, the European Union has expressed its interest in the Arctic Ocean, with a number of its institutions making statements (such as the European Parliament in October 2008, the European Commission in November 2008, and the

---

[18] *Associated Press*, 'US, Canada at Odds over Arctic Forum', 29 March 2009.
[19] Treaty Concerning the Archipelago of Spitsbergen, and Protocol, Paris, 9 February 1920, entry into force 14 August 1925, <http://www.austlii.edu.au/au/other/dfat/treaties/1925/10.html>.

European Council in December 2009).[20] Inspired by the 1959 Antarctic Treaty, a 2008 European Parliament resolution suggested 'that as a minimum starting-point such a treaty could at least cover the unpopulated and unclaimed area at the centre of the Arctic Ocean.'[21]

The policy statement from the European Parliament about a new treaty, however, strongly conflicts with the position of the Arctic coastal states, which asserted in their Ilulissat Declaration that they 'see no need to develop a new comprehensive international legal regime to govern the Arctic Ocean' beyond the framework of the law of the sea to which they 'remain committed.'[22] Subsequently, the European Council concluded in December 2009 that the 'EU policy on Arctic issues should be based on ... the United Nations Convention on the Law of the Sea and other relevant international instruments'.[23]

Discussions pertaining to the lessons on international co-operation and policy development garnered from the experience of Antarctica are often misconstrued as veiled attempts to discuss a new treaty for the high north. Aside from distinct differences between the Arctic and Antarctic (Table 6), discussions about a new Arctic treaty[24] also seem premature without a shared understanding between parties of the political, economic and cultural instabilities

---

[20] European Parliament Resolution on Arctic Governance, Brussels, 9 October 2008, <http://www.europarl.europa.eu/sides/getDoc.do?pubRef=-//EP//TEXT+TA+P6-TA-2008-0474+0+DOC+XML+V0//EN>. Communication from the Commission to the European Parliament and the Council, 'The European Union and the Arctic Region', 20 November 2008, <http://ec.europa.eu/external_relations/arctic_region/docs/com_08_763_en.pdf>. Council of the European Union, 'Council Conclusions on Arctic Issues', 8 December 2009, <http://www.consilium.europa.eu/ueDocs/cms_Data/docs/pressData/EN/foraff/111814.pdf>.
[21] European Parliament, *op. cit.*, 9 October 2008.
[22] Ilulissat Declaration, *op. cit.*
[23] Council of the European Union, *op. cit.* 8 December 2009.
[24] T Koivurova and E J Molenaar, 'International Governance and Regulation of the Marine Arctic: A Proposal For A Legally Binding Instrument' (Oslo: WWF International Arctic Programme, 2009).

that will emerge from the environmental state-change in the Arctic Ocean. Only after such analyses will it be possible to evaluate existing institutions to determine their efficiencies, redundancies, gaps and contradictions in responding to such instabilities. In this regard, the governance push from the European Parliament,[25] and the analyses of the gaps by other quarters,[26] demonstrates that more work is needed to determine how UNCLOS can be applied to accommodate the interests of the international community in the Arctic Ocean (Figure 11).

Set against long-standing historical norms and institutions, the 1982 UNCLOS is still in its infancy,[27] with flexibility to implement adaptation or mitigation policies for resolving the emergent instabilities in the Arctic Ocean. Policy frameworks, considered in terms of 'soft' and 'hard' law,[28] are related to landmark declarations and speeches as well as agreements and institutions that facilitate co-ordinated national implementation (Figure 13).

From the end of the Cold War to the present, international policies that apply to the Arctic Ocean further involve a spectrum of issues ranging from specific components in the Arctic marine ecosystem to human activities generally in the world ocean.[29] This includes specific institutions that focus on defined elements of the Arctic Ocean ecosystem (Figure 5), such as the 1973

---

[25] European Union, *op. cit.* in note 21.

[26] T Koivurova and E J Molenaar, 'International Governance and Regulation of the Marine Arctic: Overview and Gap Analysis' (Oslo: WWF International Arctic Programme, 2009).

[27] P A Berkman, 'President Eisenhower, the Antarctic and the Origin of International Spaces' in P A Berkman, M Lang, D W H Walton and O R Young (eds), *Science Diplomacy: Antarctica, Science and the Governance of International Spaces* (Washington, DC: Smithsonian Institution Scholarly Press, 2010 [in press]).

[28] U Mörth, *Soft Law in Governance and Regulation: An Interdisciplinary Analysis* (Cheltenham: Edward Elgar, 2004).

[29] Databases to identify dates of signature and ratification, current parties, chronologies and summaries of conventions, treaties and agreements that are relevant to the Arctic, include: <http://www.ecolex.org>; <http://nsdl.tierit.com>; <http://sedac.ciesin.columbia.edu/entri/>; and <http://untreaty.un.org/>.

Agreement on the Conservation of Polar Bears, to which the five Arctic coastal states are parties. Within the Arctic Ocean region there also are institutions that focus on activities within defined areas, such as the 1920 Treaty Concerning the Archipelago of Spitsbergen, and Protocol (Table 3).

More broadly, the Arctic Council is a high-level forum for shared dialogues about the 'common Arctic issues' of sustainable development and environmental protection in the Arctic, but without the legal personality to create binding measures. The Arctic Council reports contain meaningful data, objective analyses and insights from both international and interdisciplinary experts. Although necessary, these reports and assessments alone are insufficient. A key challenge for the Arctic Council and, more generally parties involved in Arctic governance, is to translate existing insights into operational policies that can be consistently and co-operatively applied by the diverse rights-holders (Table 3) to solve urgent issues across the Arctic Ocean.

Figure 13: *See colour plate on p. 25*

The Arctic Council is centrally positioned (Figure 11) to facilitate effective interplay among institutions and parties in a manner that will strengthen this high-level forum. Conversely, shirking this stewardship role for sovereign benefit will weaken the Arctic Council. Indeed, it seems that the Arctic Council is at a crossroads.[30]

Regional institutions can also establish regulations for commercial activities in the Arctic Ocean and its surrounds, such as the 1980 Convention on Future Multilateral Cooperation in North-East Atlantic Fisheries (NEAFC).[31] Similarly, there are regional institutions that can regulate environmental impacts, such as the 1992 Convention for the Protection of the Marine

---

[30] T Koivurova, 'Limits and Possibilities of the Arctic Council in a Rapidly Changing Scene of Arctic Governance', *Polar Record* (Vol. 46, 2008), pp. 146–56.

[31] Convention on Future Multilateral Cooperation in North-East Atlantic Fisheries, London, 18 November 1980, entry into force 17 March 1982, <http://www.neafc.org/>.

Environment of the North-East Atlantic (OSPAR).[32] Both of these institutions are in force and apply to the Arctic Ocean as well as the Northeast Atlantic (Table 3).

On a global level, there also are institutions that target specific types of human impact, such as the 1973–78 International Convention for the Prevention of Pollution from Ships,[33] and the 1995 United Nations Fish Stocks Agreement,[34] which are fully applicable to the Arctic. At the most inclusive level – as the umbrella framework for all ocean laws and policies – is the UNCLOS, as stated in the 2008 Ilulissat Declaration:[35]

> Notably, the law of the sea provides for important rights and obligations concerning the delineation of the outer limits of the continental shelf, the protection of the marine environment, including ice-covered areas, freedom of navigation, marine scientific research, and other uses of the sea.

Cost-effective, consistent and synergistic interplay among relevant organisations, forums, institutions and nations (Table 3) is a matter for visionary international stewardship in the Arctic Ocean (Figure 11).

Environmental Security Integration

Environmental security in the Arctic Ocean provides a conceptual framework to address political, economic and cultural instabilities

---

[32] Convention for the Protection of the Marine Environment of the North-East Atlantic, Paris, 22 September 1992, entry into force 25 March 1998. OSPAR emerged from its preceding Oslo and Paris conventions, <http://www.ospar.org>.

[33] Convention on the Prevention of Pollution by Ships (MARPOL), London, 2 November 1973. See the International Maritime Organisation for the MARPOL convention with its associated amendments and annexes, <http://www.imo.org>.

[34] Agreement for the Implementation of the Provisions of the United Nations Convention on the Law of the Sea Relating to the Conservation and Management of Straddling Fish Stocks and Highly Migratory Fish Stocks, New York, 4 August 1995, entry into force 11 December 2001, <http://www.fao.org/fishery/topic/13701/en>.

[35] *Ilulissat Declaration, op. cit.*

that will impact states and indigenous peoples in the high north as well as the global community (Figure 11). What makes this concept distinctive is the recognition that environmental issues increasingly pose threats to security, as the European Commission stated in its November 2008 communication:[36]

> In view of the role of climate change as a 'threats multiplier' ... environmental changes are altering geo-strategic dynamics of the Arctic with potential consequences for international stability.

There are a wide range of considerations in the Arctic Ocean – energy, shipping, fisheries and other commercial activities, which are integrated with military aspects – that require shared solutions.[37] Beyond notions of 'hard security' or 'soft security',[38] **the overriding challenge in the Arctic Ocean is to balance national and common interests, recognising that states will always put their own interests first and foremost.**

States are individually addressing their own security interests in the Arctic, as illustrated most prominently by the State Policy of the Russian Federation in the Arctic Until 2020 that was adopted by President Dmitry Medvedev in September 2008,[39] and the United States' Arctic Region Policy that was signed by President George W Bush in January 2009.[40] National security strategies also have been issued from the other Arctic coastal states Norway,[41] Canada[42] and

---

[36] European Union, *op. cit.*

[37] K Zysk, 'Russia and the High North: Security and Defence Perspectives' in S G Holtsmark and B A Smith-Windsor (eds), *Security Prospects in the High North: Geostrategic Thaw or Freeze?* (Rome: NATO Defense College, 2009), pp. 102–29.

[38] C Archer, 'Security Prospects in the High North and the United Kingdom' in Holtsmark and Smith-Windsor, *op. cit.*

[39] Basics of the State Policy of the Russian Federation, *op. cit.*

[40] United States National Security Presidential Directive 66, *op. cit.*

[41] Norwegian Ministry of Foreign Affairs, The Norwegian Government's High North Strategy, 1 December 2006.

[42] Government of Canada, 'Canada's Northern Strategy: Our North, Our Heritage, Our Future', 2009, <http://www.northernstrategy.ca/cns/cns.pdf>.

Table 10: Transboundary Interests in the National Security Policies of the Arctic Coastal States.[a]

Arctic Coastal State	Terms that reflect transboundary interests					
	Peace and Stability	Environment	Indigenous (Peoples)	Transport/ Shipping	Fisheries	Science and Technology
Canada		X	X	X	X	X
Denmark	X	X	X	X	X	X
Norway	X	X	X	X	X	X
Russian Federation	X	X	X	X	X	X
United States		X	X	X	X	X

[a] Based on full-text searching of national security documents and explicit use of terms that are related to transboundary issues. This excludes other transboundary issues such as energy, minerals and military ones.

Denmark.[43] Beyond military and defence topics (which also are included), these national security policies further reveal the transboundary interests of states in the Arctic Ocean.

These transboundary security interests are mapped between the national policies of the Arctic coastal states, based on the explicit context of terms that are used (Table 10). For example, the 2009 State Policy of the Russian Federation in the Arctic Until 2020 refers to the 'maintenance of the Arctic as a zone of peace and cooperation' and the 'maintenance of the peace and stability in the Arctic region.' In contrast, the 2009 United States' Arctic Region Policy only encourages 'the peaceful resolution of disputes in the Arctic region.' Consequently, peace and stability in the Arctic Ocean are not considered to be explicit goals of the United States' national security policy for the region.

Groups of Arctic nations and peoples also are expressing their security interests in the Arctic. The Nordic countries of Denmark, Finland, Iceland, Norway and Sweden have expressed their solidarity for peace-building, air surveillance, maritime monitoring, societal security, foreign service and military co-operation in the Arctic.[44] In addition to declaring the sovereignty of Inuit peoples, the Circumpolar Inuit Council has asserted its interests in 'environmental security'.[45]

Denmark, Finland and Sweden are members of the European Union, which has declared the 'EU should work to uphold the further development of a co-operative Arctic governance system based on the UNCLOS which would ensure: security and stability; strict environmental management, including respect of the precautionary principle; sustainable use of

---

[43] Namminersornerullutik Oqartussat Udenrigsministeriet, *Arktis i en Brydningstid Forslag til Strategi for Aktiviteter i det Arktiske Område*, May 2008 (in Danish).

[44] T Stoltenberg, 'Nordic Cooperation on Foreign and Security Policy', Proposals Presented to the Extraordinary Meeting of Nordic Foreign Ministers, Oslo, 9 February 2009.

[45] Circumpolar Inuit Declaration on Arctic Sovereignty, adopted by the Inuit Circumpolar Council on behalf of the Inuit in Greenland, Canada, Alaska, and Chukotka, 28 April 2009, <http://www.itk.ca/circumpolar-inuit-declaration-arctic-sovereignty>.

resources as well as open and equitable access'.[46] With the notable exception of the Russian Federation, the four other Arctic coastal states, along with Iceland and other members of NATO, have also begun exploring:[47]

> issues that could be construed as dimensions of future Arctic security. They are divided into four groups: military and territorial security; environmental security; economic, energy and functional security; and the remaining 'human security' issues.

Relations with Russia

Even though the Russian Federation is excluded from the alliance, NATO does consider the 'crucial role of the United States and Russia for Arctic stability and prosperity', as stated at its January 2009 Arctic security meeting in Reykjavik, Iceland.[48] With this in view, it has further been suggested that:[49]

> Western policy makers should set for themselves the ambitious aim of developing the High North into a source of stability, community of interest and cooperation between Russia and the West. The same applies to their Russian counterparts. The two sides ought to shift their focus from tactical differences to desired end states and shared objectives. The Arctic Ocean area, where numerous arenas for comprehensive cooperation are still open, represents a chance to put these guidelines into practice.

The challenge is to overcome long-standing distrust between Russia and NATO, as reflected by the February 2010 Russian Military Doctrine:[50]

---

[46] Communication from the Commission to the European Parliament and the Council, *op. cit.*
[47] Holtsmark and Smith-Windsor, *op. cit.*
[48] *Ibid.*
[49] S G Holtsmark, *Cooperation Rather than Confrontation: Security in the High North,* Research Briefing (Rome: NATO Defense College, 2009), p. 8.
[50] President Dmitri Medvedev, 'Military Doctrine of Russia', 5 February 2010, <http://www.scrf.gov.ru/documents/33.html> (in Russian).

The main external threat of war: a) the desire to give the power potential of the North Atlantic Treaty Organization (NATO), global functions, implemented in violation of international law, to bring the military infrastructure of the countries – members of NATO to the borders of Russia, including through the expansion of the bloc.

As actions justified in terms of national security become more prominent throughout the Arctic (Table 10), the injunction of the 1996 Ottawa Declaration that the Arctic Council 'should not deal with matters related to military security'[51] has emerged as a serious constraint on efforts to design a coherent and integrated approach to Arctic Ocean stewardship. This has not precluded separate measures directed towards specific military security issues, such as AMEC's programme to mitigate impacts of radioactive waste associated with decommissioned nuclear submarines,[52] but it has truncated efforts to address security concepts regarding the Arctic Ocean in a shared context.

Even though issues of military security and energy security are divisive, Russia's Arctic state policy does make efforts to suggest common ground in the 'sphere of environmental security', in:[53]

> preservation and maintenance of environment protection of the Arctic, liquidation of ecological consequences of economic activities in the conditions of increasing economic activity and global changes of climate.

Security and UNCLOS

The Arctic Council alone is not the answer, but it does offer a locus for networking among existing institutions that are relevant to environmental security in the Arctic Ocean (see Figure 13). The solution is to utilise the law of the sea as an extensive international

---

[51] Declaration on the Establishment of the Arctic Council, Ottawa, 19 September 1996.

[52] Declaration among the Department of Defense of the United States of America, the Royal Ministry of Defence of the Kingdom of Norway, and the Ministry of Defence of the Russian Federation, on Arctic Military Environmental Cooperation, Bergen, 26 September 1996.

[53] Basics of the State Policy of the Russian Federation, *op. cit.*

legal framework to which all Arctic coastal states 'remain committed',[54] without the need to create new regimes.[55]

UNCLOS is the key to the law of the sea because it frames the conduct, responsibilities and rights of diverse stakeholders with regard to national and international zones extending seaward from coastal baselines (Figure 12). Even though it has yet to adopt UNCLOS, especially with regard to provisions for the 'common heritage of mankind' in the area of the deep sea, the United States does accept these sea zones under customary international law.

UNCLOS establishes institutions that are already operational in the Arctic Ocean, most prominently the Commission on the Limits of the Continental Shelf that is being applied by Russia, Norway, Iceland and Denmark to extend their continental shelf delimitations in the Arctic Ocean. UNCLOS also provides a framework for 'networked governance'[56] among existing institutions that are relevant to the Arctic, including those involved with the IMO and others identified in Figure 13. Importantly, with regard to environmental security, the preamble of the UNCLOS states that:

> this Convention will contribute to the strengthening of peace, security, co-operation and friendly relations among all nations in conformity with the principles of justice and equal rights and will promote the economic and social advancement of all peoples of the world...

Overall, security is mentioned in seventeen different UNCLOS articles.[57] For example, Article 19 states that 'passage is innocent so long as it is not prejudicial to the peace, good order or security of the coastal State'. The security interests and rights of coastal States are elaborated with regard to innocent passage in Article 25:

---

[54] Ilulissat Declaration. *op. cit.*
[55] O R Young, *Creating Regimes: Arctic Accords and International Governance* (Ithaca: Cornell University Press, 1998).
[56] See the Program on Networked Governance, John F Kennedy School of Government, Harvard University, <http://www.hks.harvard.edu/netgov/html/index.htm>
[57] Terms such as 'security' in the UNCLOS can be comprehensively searched via the database at EvREsearch Ltd, *op. cit.*

> The coastal State may, without discrimination in form or in fact among foreign ships, suspend temporarily in specified areas of its territorial sea the innocent passage of foreign ships if such suspension is essential for the protection of its security, including weapons exercises.

Similarly, Article 52 elaborates the security interests and rights of archipelagic states with regard to innocent passage:

> The archipelagic State may, without discrimination in form or in fact among foreign ships, suspend temporarily in specified areas of its archipelagic waters the innocent passage of foreign ships if such suspension is essential for the protection of its security. Such suspension shall take effect only after having been duly published.

Security is further mentioned in Article 138 with regard to the deep sea:

> The general conduct of States in relation to the Area shall be in accordance with the provisions of this Part, the principles embodied in the Charter of the United Nations and other rules of international law in the interests of maintaining peace and security and promoting international co-operation and mutual understanding.

UNCLOS Article 298 further involves provisions to co-ordinate with the UN Security Council to resolve disputes concerning military activities in the sea. Security is also a component of the general provisions of UNCLOS as stated in Article 302. These references illustrate opportunities for the international community to utilise UNCLOS as a framework for addressing security issues in a manner that has been avoided in the Arctic Ocean.

To assure future Arctic security, trust must be built amongst all the coastal states of the Arctic Ocean. Stewardship responsibilities of the Arctic coastal states are beyond question (Figure 11); the Arctic Ocean is in their backyards.[58]

> The effects of climate on the Arctic Ocean are dramatic. All states, and in particular the Arctic states, have a shared responsibility to protect the Arctic Ocean against irreversible damages to the ecosystems.

---

[58] Støre, *op. cit.*

The question is whether the Arctic coastal states will go beyond just assessing impact, and truly stand together and provide the stewardship needed to implement measures that will ensure that the Arctic Ocean and its ecosystems are protected as a matter of urgency. In the words of the UN:[59]

> The nation state is insufficient to deal with threats to shared ecosystems. Threats to environmental security can only be dealt with by joint management and multilateral procedures and mechanisms.

In addition to providing a template for addressing the risks of potential political, economic and cultural instabilities in an integrated manner, environmental security provides both a tangible basis and a policy template to balance national and common interests in the Arctic Ocean:[60]

> The notion of environmental security is particularly relevant to the Arctic, for several reasons. The first concerns the fragility of northern ecosystems and their extreme vulnerability to any human disturbance. Second, the area has a profound influence upon global (or at least hemispheric) environmental processes, such as atmospheric and ocean circulation, global warming, and ozone layer depletion. Finally, environmental factors are closely linked to longstanding, but now changing, strategic military objectives in the Arctic.

As concluded from the 2009 Arctic Climate Change and Security Policy Conference, 'Arctic environmental security should receive priority attention as the key regional security issue'.[61]

---

[59] United Nations World Commission on Environment and Development, *Our Common Future* (Oxford: Oxford University Press, 1987), <http://www.un-documents.net/wced-ocf.htm>.

[60] J M Broadus and R V Vartanov, *Oceans and Environmental Security: Shared US and Russian Perspectives* (Washington, DC: Island Press, 1994).

[61] K S Yalowitz, J F Collins and R A Virginia, *The Arctic Climate Change and Security Policy Conference – Final Report and Findings* (Dartmouth: Carnegie Endowment for International Peace, 2009), <http://www.carnegieendowment.org/files/arctic_climate_change.pdf>.

National–International Balance

To achieve stewardship in the Arctic Ocean, the challenge is to balance interests, rights and responsibilities across as well as beyond sovereign jurisdictions. On the sea floor, beyond the continental shelf, rise and slope, is the deep sea. The deep sea is universally accepted as an international space beyond national jurisdictions (Table 5).

However, where the deep sea begins is an intense question that is being addressed around the world by the Commission on the Limits of the Continental Shelf as provided by UNCLOS Article 76.[62] The Russian Federation (2001), Norway (2006), Iceland (2009) and Denmark (2009) have already submitted proposals to the Commission to extend their continental shelves north in the Arctic Ocean. Such proposals and activities, including the 2007 public-private expedition to plant a Russian flag on the sea floor at the North Pole,[63] are driving wedges between the Arctic coastal states as the world watches the Arctic Ocean sliced into pieces of a geopolitical pie (Figure 14).

Figure 14: *See colour plate on p. 26*

Another complication with the deep sea is the possible exploitation of its mineral resources, stemming from the concepts introduced by the Maltese ambassador to the UN, Arvid Pardo, on 1 November 1967:[64]

> The seabed and the ocean floor are a common heritage of mankind and should be used and exploited for peaceful purposes and for the exclusive benefit of mankind as a whole. The needs of poor countries, representing that part of mankind which is most in need

---

[62] Submissions to the Commission on the Limits of the Continental Shelf as provided by UNCLOS Article 76, <http://www.un.org/Depts/los/clcs_new/clcs_home.htm>.

[63] A Revkin, 'Russians Plant Flag on the Arctic Seabed', *New York Times*, 3 August 2007.

[64] United Nations General Assembly, 'Examination of the question of the reservation exclusively for peaceful purposes of the seabed and the ocean floor, and the subsoil thereof, underlying the High seas beyond the limits of present national jurisdiction, and the use of their resources in the interests of mankind', Agenda item 92, 1 November 1967.

of assistance, should receive preferential consideration in the event of financial benefits being derived from the exploitation of the seabed and ocean floor for commercial purposes.

The following year, the UN adopted Resolution 2467 (XXIII),[65] which established the Committee on the Peaceful Uses of the Sea-Bed and Ocean Floor Beyond the Limits of National Jurisdictions, composed of the USSR, UK and US, as well as thirty-nine other states. One of the products of this UN committee was the 1971 Treaty on the Prohibition of the Emplacement of Nuclear Weapons and Other Weapons of Mass Destruction on the Seabed and the Ocean Floor and in the Subsoil Thereof (see Table 5). There remains, however, disagreement among a few nations about the 'common heritage of mankind' concept that was introduced in the UN in 1967. Most notably, because of economic and technical reasons associated with exploiting mineral resources in the international 'area' of the deep sea, the United States has not ratified UNCLOS.[66]

Sovereignty, sovereign rights and jurisdiction of coastal states in the Arctic Ocean are reflected by the law of the sea zones that are identified in the presidential policies issued in 2009 by the United States:[67]

> [S]overeignty, sovereign rights, and jurisdiction in the Arctic region, including sovereignty within the territorial sea, sovereign rights and jurisdiction within the United States exclusive economic zone and on the continental shelf, and appropriate control in the United States contiguous zone

---

[65] United Nations General Assembly, 'Examination of the question of the reservation exclusively for peaceful purposes of the sea-bed and the ocean floor, and the subsoil thereof, underlying the High seas beyond the limits of present national jurisdiction, and the use of their resources in the interests of mankind', Resolution 2467 (XXIII), 19 December 1968.

[66] P M Leitner, 'A Bad Treaty Returns: The Case of the Law of the Sea Treaty', *World Affairs* (Vol. 160, 1998), pp. 134–50.

[67] National Security Presidential Directive 66, *op. cit.*; Homeland Security Presidential Directive 25, 9 January 2009.

And the Russian Federation:[68]

> [I]nternal maritime waters, territorial sea, exclusive economic zone and continental shelf of the Russian Federation adjoining to such territories, areas and islands, within which Russia enjoys sovereign rights and jurisdiction under international law.

Both the United States and the Russian Federation are asserting their national interests through the EEZ and across the continental shelf. Even though the outer continental shelf may eventually include the sea floor that currently is defined as the deep sea – in some areas, potentially all the way to the North Pole – neither of these coastal states nor any other states have incorporated the international spaces (Table 5) of either the deep sea or the high seas into their national policies.

The question still remains about how to balance national and common interests in the Arctic Ocean. Moreover, 'national implementation'[69] strategies lack the consistency needed to resolve transboundary impacts in a dynamic natural system. A starting place for such balance exists with regions that are unambiguously and inexorably beyond sovereign jurisdictions.

A first principle is that the sea floor (much of which may well come under coastal state jurisdiction once UNCLOS Article 76 process is complete) is legally and ecologically distinct from the overlying water column seaward of the EEZ. Consequently, the high seas surrounding the North Pole in the central Arctic Ocean will remain an international space (Figure 15), where Arctic and non-Arctic states alike (Figure 11) already share in the stewardship under the law of the sea framework.

Figure 15: *See colour plate on p. 27*

Arctic Ocean stewardship requires balanced perspectives. The coastal states have central rights and responsibilities in the Arctic Ocean (Figure 11) derived from their jurisdictions towards the North Pole (Table 10). The international community has rights

---

[68] Basics of the State Policy of the Russian Federation, *op. cit.*
[69] Ilulissat Declaration, *op. cit.*

and responsibilities in the Arctic Ocean from the high seas as an international space, outward from the North Pole toward the coastal periphery (Table 5, Figure 15). **The dichotomy of rights and responsibilities in the Arctic Ocean, as established by the law of the sea (Figure 12), underscores the challenge of balancing national interests and common interests to achieve stewardship in this globally relevant region.**

6. GLOBAL STATESMANSHIP

The Arctic Ocean is surrounded by five coastal states that have stewardship responsibilities in this globally relevant region (Figure 11). There is co-operation among diverse organisations (Table 3) to assess the complexities of the natural system, human impacts and opportunities emerging from the environmental state-change in the Arctic Ocean. There also is commitment to the law of the sea as the umbrella framework to address international interactions in the Arctic Ocean (Figures 12 and 13). While necessary, these elements are insufficient for shared responses to mitigate and adapt to the political, economic and cultural instabilities that will emerge as the permanent sea-ice cap is transformed into a seasonally ice-free sea at the top of the Earth.

The missing ingredient is statesmanship by the leaders of nations who are the only individuals that can establish the political will to both promote co-operation and prevent conflict in the Arctic Ocean for the lasting benefit of all. Such statesmanship – the ability to extinguish the brush fires of the moment and the vision to offer hope for future generations – appears rarely.

Addressing security issues in the Arctic Ocean is not about opening a new 'great game'[1] in the high north. Indeed, cat-and-mouse submarine deployments under the Arctic sea-ice cap have been uninterrupted since the end of the Cold War,[2] and there has been ongoing SLBM testing in the Arctic Ocean since

---

[1] S G Borgerson, 'The Great Game Moves North: As the Arctic Melts, Countries Vie for Control', *Foreign Affairs* (March 2009).

[2] E Miasnikov, 'Submarine Collision off Murmansk: A Look from Afar', *Breakthrough* (Vol. 2, No. 2, 1993), pp. 19–24.

the early 1960s (Figure 8). Moreover, Cold War-type threats are still perceived to persist: the Russian Federation's 'main external threat of war', for instance, is seen as involving 'members of NATO to the borders of Russia, including through the expansion of the bloc.'[3] Without being either alarmist or alarming,[4] the reality is that Cold War mindsets have been frozen in the Arctic Ocean, and shared security strategies have not evolved between the United States and Russian Federation. As observed by Hans Corell, Legal Counsel of the United Nations from 1994–2004:[5]

> Good relations between Moscow and Washington are imperative for a more positive development in the field of international peace and security. The unfortunate tensions that have developed between the two major powers bordering the Arctic simply must be removed, and this can be achieved only through a demonstration of statesmanship on both sides.

In this 'age of the Arctic'[6] – in the midst of spiralling international urgencies – 'matters relating to the Arctic and the High North must be addressed at the highest political level'.[7] Building on the remarks by Secretary of State Hillary Clinton at the first joint meeting of the Arctic Council and Antarctic Treaty Consultative Parties in 2009,[8] it is important to ask: **what is the**

---

[3] President Dmitri Medvedev, 'Military Doctrine of Russia', 5 February 2010, <http://news.kremlin.ru/ref_notes/461>.

[4] O R Young, 'Whither the Arctic? Conflict or Cooperation in the Circumpolar North', *Polar Record* (Vol. 45, 2009), pp. 73–82.

[5] H Corell, 'The Arctic: An Opportunity to Cooperate and Demonstrate International Statesmanship', *Venderbilit Journal of Transnational Law* (Vol. 42, No. 4, 2009), pp. 1065–79.

[6] O R Young, 'The Age of the Arctic', *Foreign Policy* (Vol. 61, 1986), pp.160–79; G Osherenko and O R Young, *The Age of the Arctic: Hot Conflicts and Cold Realities* (Cambridge: Cambridge University Press, 1989).

[7] H Corell, *Conclusions: Common Concern for the Arctic. An Arctic Conference Organized by the Nordic Council of Ministers*, 9–10 September 2008 (Greenland: Ilulissat, 2008), <http://www.havc.se/res/SelectedMaterial/20080910chairmansconclusions.pdf>.

[8] Secretary of State Hillary Clinton, 'Remarks at The Joint Session of the Antarctic Treaty Consultative Meeting and the Arctic Council, 50th

path to 'strengthen peace and security, and support sustainable economic development, and protect the environment' in the Arctic Ocean?

To avoid the 'tragedy of the commons',[9] a first step in this journey is to build on the 'common Arctic issues' of sustainable development and environmental protection identified in the 1996 Ottawa Declaration that established the Arctic Council.[10] Sustainable development provides a unifying platform to balance economic prosperity, social equity and environmental protection. The difficulty with sustainable development is that it projects solutions into the future, which is anathema to governments that must constantly react to urgent issues of the moment. For governments, prioritising the allocation of available resources is a security matter, necessary to resolve risks that jeopardise their economic, cultural and political stability.

What is the alignment between security and sustainable development? In a general sense, security involves risks of economic, cultural and political instabilities from the urgent allocation of resources. Sustainable development similarly focuses on economic prosperity and social equity, but with progressive allocation of resources and environmental protection as a key component.[11] As noted by the United Nations World Commission on Environment and Development:[12]

> The first step in creating a more satisfactory basis for managing the interrelationships between security and sustainable development is to broaden our vision. Conflicts may arise not only because of

---

Anniversary of the Antarctic Treaty', Washington, DC, 6 April 2009, <http://www.state.gov/secretary/rm/2009a/04/121314.htm>.

[9] G Hardin, 'Tragedy of the Commons', *Science* (Vol. 162, 1968), pp. 1, 243–48.

[10] Declaration on the Establishment of the Arctic Council, Ottawa, 19 September 1996, <http://www.international.gc.ca/polar-polaire/ottdec-decott.aspx>.

[11] M Tennberg, *Arctic Environmental Cooperation: A Study in Governmentality* (Burlington: Ashgate, 2000).

[12] United Nations World Commission on Environment and Development, *Our Common Future* (Oxford: Oxford University Press, 1987), <http://www.un-documents.net/wced-ocf.htm>.

political and military threats to national sovereignty; they may derive also from environmental degradation and the pre-emption of development options.

In the Arctic Ocean, the alignment will also come with the application of environmental security as an element of sustainable development[13] to address urgent risks of instabilities arising from the environmental state-change (Figure 3). As observed by Achim Steiner, Director of the United Nations Environment Programme:[14]

> All these issues – from energy security and climate security, to water and health security – are ultimately just part of a far wider issue not only for this but for generations to come, namely environmental security.

The Arctic Ocean involves a complexity of physical (Figures 1, 3 and 5) and biological (Figure 6) phenomena with the superimposition of human activities (Figures 2 and 9). Its vast potential for energy extraction and living resources, a burgeoning trade route that will impact the global balance of power, intensifying interests from non-Arctic states – especially the European Union (Figure 13) and China,[15] and ongoing Cold War legacy of strategic nuclear assets (Figure 8), all in a confined area that involves sovereign jurisdictions as well as international spaces (Figures 14 and 15) makes the Arctic Ocean a unique marine region that will establish global precedents for future generations.

The notion of contributing to future generations is more tangible today than any other time in human history. We now can look across centuries and millennia to understand the relevance of modern events and phenomena. With current technologies, we have an unprecedented ability to look back through time across societies and empires with empirical evidence about their interactions with environments of the past. We also have an

---

[13] *Ibid.*

[14] A Steiner, 'Environmental Security' in Maurice Fraser (ed.), *G8 Summit 2006: Issues and Instruments* (Newsdesk Media Group, 2006), pp. 52–56, <http://www.g8.utoronto.ca/newsdesk/g8-2006.html>.

[15] L Jakobson, 'China Prepares for an Ice-free Arctic', *SIPRI Insights on Peace and Security* (Vol. 2, 2010), pp. 1–14, <http://books.sipri.org/files/insight/SIPRIInsight1002.pdf>.

expanding capacity to predict future environmental conditions and impacts in our world (for instance, see Figure 3), reflecting the increasing dependence of decision-making on good science. In this civilisational context, the establishment of international spaces is still in its infancy, having happened only in the past fifty years with globally recognised institutions that apply to environments and ecosystems beyond sovereign jurisdictions (Table 5).

The Arctic Ocean is being transformed into a global trade route that will involve sea lanes, ports, and administration facilities along with communication, tariff, monitoring and forecasting systems. There will be assets that can be deployed quickly for diverse vessel emergencies. There will be new networks to transport resources and commerce southward across continents. Such maritime spatial planning[16] is like that of the early twentieth century when nations recognised that they would need to accommodate the traffic from a car in every home, projecting vast grids of paved roads and highways that would take the next fifty years to construct. As noted by President Theodore Roosevelt at the National and International Roads Convention in 1903:[17]

> When we wish to use descriptive terms fit to characterize great empires ... invariably one of the terms used is to signify that that empire built good roads. When we speak of the Romans, we speak of them as rulers, as conquerors, as administrators, as road-builders.

The complication in the Arctic Ocean is that such infrastructure will be a shared enterprise of all the Arctic coastal states (Figure 11), together with involvement from many other states and investment from additional stakeholders. The challenge will be to manage escalating competition and demand for

---

[16] European Commission, 'Roadmap for Maritime Spatial Planning: Achieving Common Principles in the EU', 25 November 2008, <http://ec.europa.eu/maritimeaffairs/spatial_planning_en.html>.

[17] President Theodore Roosevelt 'Address in St. Louis, Missouri to the National and International Good Roads Convention, 29 April 1903' in *Address and Presidential Message of Theodore Roosevelt, 1902–1904* (New York: G P Putnam's Sons, 1904).

resources in the Arctic Ocean. Moreover, as a warning from the 1980s that is clearly relevant to the Arctic Ocean today:[18]

> Conflict over resources is likely to grow more intense as demand for some essential commodities increases and supplies appear more precarious. These conflicts will also have their territorial aspects, of course, but the territory in contention is likely either to be unpopulated or only sparsely populated. Much of it will be under water – oil-rich portions of the continental shelves.

There is no magic bullet to prepare for the Arctic Ocean's transformation. Along the way there will be political, economic, cultural and environmental instabilities; some that can be predicted, while others will be unanticipated. The challenge is to establish a process that is international, interdisciplinary and inclusive. This process, in many ways, could be conducted through the high-level forum of the Arctic Council.

However, the Arctic Council is precluded from dealing with 'matters related to military security', which has translated operationally into its avoidance of any security matters. Nonetheless, the environmental state-change in the Arctic Ocean is a security matter that will 'require a fundamentally different approach to the planning, technology, and deployment of security assets'.[19] Environmental security is broader than military security and it complements the 'common Arctic issues' in the 1996 Ottawa Declaration that established the Arctic Council.

Peace as a Common Interest
Fundamentally, the established 'common issues' reflect an understanding of shared interests among the Arctic states, indigenous peoples and other stakeholders regarding the Arctic Ocean (Figure 11). However, the 'common Arctic issues' are incomplete. Explicit use of the term 'peace' as a common interest in the 1996 Ottawa Declaration was specifically excluded. This

---

[18] R H Ullman, 'Redefining Security', *International Security* (Vol. 8, No. 1, 1983), pp. 129–53.
[19] G A Backus and J H Strickland, *Climate-Derived Tensions in Arctic Security* (Oak Ridge: Sandia National Laboratories, 2008), <http://est.sandia.gov/earth/docs/Tensions_in_Arctic_SecurityFinal.pdf>.

position remains unchanged, as reflected in the 2008 Ilulissat Declaration[20] of the five Arctic coastal states, in which they promoted their 'stewardship role' without explicitly identifying peace as a common interest in the Arctic region.

This is not to say that the Arctic states are interested in conflict, nor that peace is excluded in all declarations. For example, the 2009 Tromsø Declaration of the Arctic Council confirms 'that in international relations the rule of law is a prerequisite for peaceful regional development'.[21] However, peace and stability in the Arctic region have yet to be identified explicitly as national security objectives of all Arctic states (Table 10).

What is the strategy needed to elevate 'Arctic international relations from the official to the highest political level'?[22] **Where is the leadership of heads of state to both promote co-operation and prevent conflict as risks of instabilities emerge with the environmental state-change in the Arctic Ocean?** A tangible step would be for heads of state to establish peace in the Arctic Ocean as an explicit common interest.

As an international space (Table 5, Figure 12), the high seas opens a door to address the Arctic interests of all nations now into the distant future. The high seas are defined and delimited without dispute in the central Arctic Ocean beyond the exclusive economic zones (Figure 15), accepted by all states either as parties of UNCLOS or through customary international

---

[20] The Ilulissat Declaration from the Arctic Ocean Conference, Ilulissat, Greenland, 28 May 2008, <http://www.oceanlaw.org/downloads/arctic/Ilulissat_Declaration.pdf>.
[21] 'Tromsø Declaration', Sixth Ministerial Meeting of the Arctic Council, Tromsø, Norway, 29 April 2009 <http://arctic-council.org/filearchive/Tromsoe%20Declaration-1.pdf>.
[22] F Griffiths, *Towards a Canadian Arctic Strategy: Foreign Policy for Canada's Tomorrow*, No. 1 (Ontario: Canadian International Council, 2009).

law.[23] Moreover, the high seas are legally distinct from the sea floor (Figure 14), even if the Commission on the Limits on the Continental Shelf approves shelf extensions all the way to the North Pole.

As reflected by the 2009 Arctic policies of the United States and the Russian Federation, national security is defined by areas under their jurisdiction running from their coastal baselines to the outer edge of the EEZ with inclusion of the territorial sea, contiguous zone and continental shelf. A polar perspective emphasising the area beyond national jurisdiction, by contrast, grants national leaders an unobstructed opportunity to elaborate their common interests:[24]

> Peacefully resolving the overriding political, economic and social concerns of our time requires a multifaceted approach, including mechanisms to address the links between the natural environment and human security.

Consider that a nation's security is directly proportional to its bushel of policy options based on national interests that can be deployed at any moment. If policy options are removed, after all diplomatic channels have been exhausted, at the end of the tunnel is conflict. Conversely, if a nation can add policy options derived from common interests, it will expand its capacity to respond to urgent issues thereby enhancing its stability: 'security increases as vulnerability decreases'.[25]

---

[23] A Vylegzhanin, 'Developing International Law Teachings for Preventing Inter-state Disaccords in the Arctic Ocean' in G Witschel, I Winkelmann, K Tiroch and R Wolfrum (eds), *New Chances and New Responsibilities in the Arctic Region* (Berlin: Berliner Wissenschafts-Verlag, 2009), pp. 209–22.

[24] Such as via the combined international initiative, the Environment and Security Initiative, in which a number of international organisations have joined forces, including the UNDP, UNEP, OSCE, NATO, Regional Environmental Center for Central and Eastern Europe (REC) and United Nations Economic Commission for Europe (UNECE), <http://www.envsec.org>.

[25] R H Ullman, 'Redefining Security', *International Security* (Vol. 8, No. 1, 1983), pp.129–53.

Balancing national interests and common interests – as illustrated by the sea floor within existing or proposed sovereign jurisdictions (Figure 14) and the high seas beyond sovereign jurisdictions (Figure 15) in the Arctic Ocean – will enhance a nation's security because it expands the 'range of policy choices available to the government of a state or to private non-governmental entities (persons, groups, corporations) within the state'.[26]

For the Arctic coastal states – which will always consider their security first and foremost – environmental security can be justified in terms of national interests, such as the Arctic state policy of the Russian Federation. For each coastal state, the combination of national interests within sovereign jurisdictions (Figure 12) plus common interests in the international space of the high seas (Figure 13) can also be justified as an expansion of policy options that will enhance their own security.

Responding to the environmental challenges and opportunities in the Arctic Ocean involves interdependencies among a suite of international and transnational organisations (Table 3) as well as among Arctic and non-Arctic nations and indigenous peoples. The importance of the high seas in the central Arctic is that it necessarily includes the entire international community in its governance under the law of the sea, to which the Arctic coastal states 'remain committed'.

As a path of least resistance, the existing framework of the high seas provides a strategy to accommodate the interests of the international community (Figure 11) without contravening the 'sovereignty, sovereign rights and jurisdiction' of the Arctic coastal states:[27]

> Before sectoral activities accelerate with the diminished sea ice, the window of opportunity is open for all legitimate stakeholders to forever establish their common interests in the central Arctic Ocean as an international space dedicated to peaceful uses.

---

[26] *Ibid.*
[27] P A Berkman and O R Young, 'Governance and Environmental Change in the Arctic Ocean', *Science* (Vol. 324, 2009), pp. 339–40.

Peaceful use of the Arctic Ocean does not have to equate with demilitarisation or restrictions on military operations that are otherwise permitted under international law. The raison d'être for military presence is ostensibly the maintenance of peace and security in the first place. Avoiding peace as an explicit common interest of all Arctic states is inconsistent with the law of the sea to which they all remain committed.

Decisions about the environmental security in the Arctic Ocean by our generation of leadership will have lasting consequences, both in the high north and globally: 'The changes underway in the Arctic will have long-term impacts on our economic future, our energy future, and indeed, again, the future of our planet'.[28]

In particular, Arctic coastal states have a responsibility to explicitly establish peace as a common interest in the Arctic Ocean; anything short of this will indicate disingenuous stewardship on their part. With the high legacy value, this is an easy way for current leaders to demonstrate the political will needed to catalyse governments into working out the details. Such decision-making today will provide global statesmanship in the Arctic Ocean for the lasting benefit of all, just as President Eisenhower did for Antarctica.

Like President Eisenhower did for Antarctica in the 1950s, the call is for global statesmanship to establish a lasting legacy of peace, stability and security in the Arctic. As noted since the Second World War, 'in view is the peace and independence of the state, not its territorial expansion or the aggrandizement of its power at the expense of the rest of the world'.[29] Building on the vision that President Gorbachev offered in 1987, with the high seas as uncontested international space in the central Arctic Ocean: **Let the North Pole become the next pole of peace**.

---

[28] Secretary of State Hillary Clinton, *op. cit.*
[29] N J Sykman, *The Geography of the Peace* (New York: Harcourt, Brace and Company, 1944).